THESE
THREE

THESE THREE

THE THEOLOGICAL VIRTUES OF FAITH, HOPE, AND LOVE

Elaine A. Robinson

THE
PILGRIM
PRESS
Cleveland

To
Ethan and Henry,
pure grace in my life,
and
the communities who have shaped me
in faith, hope, and love.

The Pilgrim Press
700 Prospect Avenue
Cleveland, Ohio 44115-1100
pilgrimpress.com

Printed in the United States of America on acid-free paper

09   08   07   06   05   04   5   4   3   2   1

Library of Congress Cataloging-in-Publication Data
Robinson, Elaine A., 1959-
    These three : the theological virtues of faith, hope, and love /
Elaine A. Robinson.
        p.   cm.
    Includes bibliographical references and index.
    ISBN 0-8298-1597-X (pbk. : alk. paper)
    1. Theological virtues. 2. Christian life – United States.   I. Title.
BV4635.R63   2004
261′.4 – dc22
                                                          2003069044

CONTENTS

FOREWORD

These Three: The Theological Virtues of Faith, Hope, and Love is a travel companion for those on the Christian path in the contemporary world. The book does not offer obtuse methodological debates or cuddly spiritual assurances. It is not easily categorized as academic theology or popular religious spirituality. Rather, with power and grace, the book provides pathways for Christians to live in a radical relation to God, others, and the world. Elaine Robinson maps for us a Christian vision of human flourishing. It is a vision lived in community and cultivated through practices, fed by the wisdom and witness of biblical stories, and expressed daily across a life lived fully, in acts of God's justice in the world.

Perhaps because the purity of Robinson's intent is so focused on giving assistance to Christians who travel the time and space of the contemporary world, she helps us to look boldly and starkly at the world in which we live. Beginning with a reflection on how our coming together on September 11 was powerful because at the fundamental, structural, cultural, and personal levels America is coming apart, the author's clarity about the contemporary world and its dis-ease is piercing. From a Christian view, she portrays a world that either fixates on the penultimacies of the self's pleasure or escapes through the timelessness of rationalization and regulation. Time and time again, she speaks of the self-absorption of contemporary life, especially for the rich, the "haves" of the world. If Americans could once be faulted for confusing nation with God, today we must confess that many Americans confuse self with God. These Americans, obsessed with increasing individual satisfaction materially and spiritually, are increasingly disengaged civically and care little about the world at large.

These Americans find an easy match in the church of consumerism: the feel-good religion of a great deal of contemporary American Christianity. In the despair of the nation, the intense poverty of the have-nots, and the destruction of the planet, some choose a course of narcissistic consumption. Others choose to submit to heteronomous authority and find rules and "rational" explanations in Christian fundamentalism as a way to deal with the dis-ease of social, personal, and earthly well-being. Here the false step is to substitute a life curtailed by a rigid, fixed ordering of security in lists of "thou shalts" and "thou shalt nots" for a life rich in relationship with God and world. This life of the spiritual automaton mistakes well-defined action for exploration of a world drenched with God. Robinson insists that "religion" posing as either a continuous gluttony of "feel good" religion or an ever-rigid checklist of religious "dos" and "do nots" has nothing to do with the God-drenched existence she wants others to explore and experience.

Robinson's context is the Protestant Christian tradition, a context with rich resources as well as an appalling decline qualitatively and qualitatively. Membership decline is a real and visible sign of the church's declining ability to reach its traditional audience in this country and help them see, hear, and know God by helping them live in community with one another and cultivate the virtues of living in relation with God. Yet in a consumerist society membership decline tends to be seen as the problem itself, not simply as a sign of it. Mega-church growth becomes the remedy for spiritual failure, and the self-absorption of religion gets fed one more time through a spiritual-type food court. Robinson wants to re-form the reformed, breaking the tradition open once again in order to be grasped by God in the midst of the world. Surely the task of breaking open Protestantism today is equal to or even greater than the task faced by earlier proclaimers such as John Huss and Martin Luther! As with earlier reformers, Robinson introduces the notion of sin as turning away from the always already ever-present grace of God. But unlike the early reformers who tend to see sin as mainly personal, Robinson also understands it as social and political.

Robinson does not linger long in analyzing these distortions of our current situation because her real interest is in helping cultivate an alternative path: the path of radical relationality that the Christian is both blessed and called to live. In the face of a bleak picture of contemporary existence, Robinson returns to classical Christian tradition, to the language of virtues, and to Trinitarian explications of faith, hope, and love to portray the Christian in radical relation to God, others, the world, and self. Many theologians speak of how Christian traditions, creatively interpreted, can speak to the world. Robinson offers us such interpretations, where the vibrancy of the traditional language of virtues meets up with fresh insights in the truth of biblical myths to move us along our journey.

Besides taking us on this journey, Robinson also moves us along in time by connecting us within the fabric of a God-drenched world. Connections and journey are the metaphors that guide this book: the connections are what hold us in the faithful journey while the journey deepens and enriches the connections. Connections and journey are interrelated for Robinson. In her reading of Genesis 2, Robinson points out that humans are created to be in full relationship with one another, with God, and with the earth. By losing this rich texture of connectedness, humans necessitate the journey toward God. Yet God is not radically only in the future or far away for Robinson: God is ever present, grasping, holding, and reaching to us on our way. The virtues — *faith, hope,* and *love* — connect us to God or, as Robinson says, they are "intertwined threads that connect us to God like an umbilical cord, unseen yet very real, providing us with nourishment and enabling us to grow to maturity and to be active, concerned citizens of both the city of God and of humanity" (p. 22). These three cultivate our relationships and form us as Christians who live in relationship with God, others, world, and self. Robinson includes with the map of each virtue details of its distortions and diseases, its nature and meaning, and its liberating demands. The journey of relation to God, and in God to world, self, and other, gives meaning and joy, but this journey demands a faithful pursuit of God's justice in the world.

Theologians have many definitions of faith including the notion that it is a sense of the whole, of being grasped, or of ultimate trust. For Robinson faith is not so much defined as it is found. Revisiting Paul Tillich's ordering of the penultimate and the ultimate and how this ordering can so easily become confused and lost, Robinson offers a fresh interpretation of the false paths of faith. Said differently: it is easy for faith to be misdirected so that knowing what faith is also requires us to attend to what it is not. Faith is misplaced if we trust science as if a God, for science and technology are always a mixture of good and bad, too intertwined with human nature to be purely good. Another heteronomous option is to trust not in science, but in the expertise of religious authority, once again elevating a penultimate authority to an ultimate one and inevitably finding dissatisfaction, if not destruction. But one can also stumble on the journey of faith by privatization, a false journey of autonomy confusing God with the individual believer. Parallel to this false path lies the one of refusing to follow the demands of faith in worship, community, or God's justice in the world. Instead, Robinson reminds us, faith is a path that comes to us as an unseen gift, an ongoing process, and a liberating demand of material transformation.

Hope and love are mapped with equal care and detail in the book. Time, space, culture, and media are refracted into hopelessness, responded to by the gift of the good life of hope — a life of hope we receive as gift and follow through our continuing testimony in freedom to God. Finally, in a powerful critique of many Christian and secular views of love, Robinson provides a subtle and sophisticated analysis of love with social, communal, and personal dimensions.

These Three: The Theological Virtues of Faith, Hope, and Love allows the reader to hear and see and feel a new way of living in a God-drenched world. How very rare and how exceedingly important is that task, that gift, and that journey.

REBECCA CHOPP
President and Professor of Philosophy
and Religion, Colgate University

ACKNOWLEDGMENTS

This project would not have been possible without the many communities and individuals who have surrounded and supported me throughout its various stages of development. First, I am grateful to my editors at The Pilgrim Press, George Graham and, especially, Ulrike Guthrie, who saw the manuscript through to completion with her participation in the creative process and her excellent editorial sensibilities. My community at Brite Divinity School has contributed in multiple ways. In particular, my thanks to Dean David Gouwens, for his support and willingness to give me some space to finish this manuscript, and to Jim Duke and Andy Lester, who provided timely and thoughtful feedback on my second and fourth chapters, respectively. My students constantly challenge me to deepen my theology, for which I am grateful, and my student assistant, Brian Eaton, has been invaluable with his superb research skills and insightful suggestions.

Beyond my academic and scholarly communities, I am deeply grateful for the friendship of my neighbors, Fred and Jill Wachter, whose door is always open and whose ears are always available, and their girls, Jasmine, Marlena, GG, and CC. In addition, a book on faith, hope, and love would be impossible without the many communities of faith who have helped me to grow in *these three*: the Cenacle Sisters in Hoschton, Georgia; the monks of Nada Hermitage in Crestone, Colorado; Academy XIV of the Academy for Spiritual Formation, where this work got its start; Sunrise UMC in Colorado Springs; Preston Hollow UMC in Dallas; the Emory University worship community; Nazareth UMC in Winder, Georgia, who taught me to be a pastor; Arlington Heights UMC in Fort Worth; and La

Trinidad Iglesia Metodista Unida in Fort Worth, *doy gracias a Dios por ustedes*. To my pastor, mentor, and friend, Ed Beck, thank you for this journey. And finally, to my boys, Ethan and Henry, who never cease to make me laugh and are a constant source of joy.

Chapter One

IS THE FABRIC FRAYED?

The tragic events of September 11, 2001, shattered the rhythm and shook the sensibilities of American life. In a few terrifying moments, thousands of lives were lost and millions of lives seemed to be changed forever. It has been said that the events of September 11 marked the loss of a sense of innocence and invulnerability that Americans previously enjoyed, raising the unavoidable question of God's presence and participation in our lives. Where is God in our contemporary turmoil? What hope have we for the future? Why believe when so much pain and suffering surrounds us? Why can't we just learn to love one another? Such questions cling to our collective psyche like a child to its parent's leg.

While the terrorist actions marked a sea change in our self-understanding and a time of serious reflection, in reality, life in the United States was difficult and troubling even before these events occurred, albeit less directly discernable or less proximate. More murders occur in the United States in one year than occurred on September 11. Violent crimes against women and children are epidemic. Hate crimes are so common that many states have introduced legislation to impose stiffer penalties. A number of recent studies document the decline in community values and the loss of a robust sense of belonging. In sum, it is not hard to believe that the social fabric of North America was unraveling long before airliners loaded with jet fuel and unwitting passengers catapulted into the twin towers of the World Trade Center, the Pentagon, and a field in Pennsylvania.

American life has been crumbling in bits and pieces for decades. We need not look beyond our own shores to discover an archaeology of loss and the tattered remnants of our social mores; the shadows of the World Trade Center merely serve as a painful and incomprehensible reminder of the violence that is too much a part of our lives, even though in far less dramatic ways on a day-to-day basis. Our extraordinary coming together as a nation on September 11 was so poignant because our ordinary patterns of life reveal that we are coming apart.

Despite the progress in legal conventions designed to protect the life, rights, and property of others, violence and individualism appear to be on the increase. Across the nation, acts of injustice and incivility intimate the deterioration of the social and moral underpinnings of society. In Cincinnati, rioting erupts following the death of an unarmed African American man at the hands of Euro-American police officers. In spite of civil rights legislation in the 1960s, America remains racially divided; all do not receive equal representation under the laws of the land. In New York City, a woman is raped and murdered in the street, as nearby tenement dwellers draw their blinds and turn up the television volume so as not to miss the game show host pronouncing, "You are the weakest link. Good-bye." In Reynosa, Mexico, U.S. multinationals erect monumental factories to injustice, where workers eke out a living at the feet of corporate America. Huddled together in the *colonias,* the shantytowns, they lack adequate housing, electricity, sanitation, running water, medical care. They are required to handle dangerous chemicals without protective clothing and breathing apparatus. They are dismissed for the smallest infraction — going to the restroom without permission or sitting down for a moment after nine or ten hours on the job. As if drawn from the pages of *The Jungle,* American corporations increase their profits on the backs of the poor and desperate, denying basic rights to those who live across borders imposed and sustained by force. Just north of the border in Texas, a woman drowns her five children; no one had seen the signs of trouble looming on the horizon or, perhaps, no one chose to intervene. In Colorado, two teenage boys stockpile an arsenal of weapons before the eyes of their families and neighbors, then execute a premeditated plan to destroy the lives of others; the more, the better. Local police forces, called to the scene, stand by in battle gear, fearing for their own safety, allowing the massacre to continue until the teenage terrorists take matters into their own hands and bring the shooting spree to an end. East and west, north and south, the fabric of American society appears dangerously close to shredding.

THE DECLINE OF AMERICAN SOCIETY

In *The American Paradox,* David G. Myers writes that since 1960, the American cultural landscape has been characterized by stunning economic gains and appalling social decline: "To an extension of Ronald Reagan's famous question, 'Are we better off than we were 40 years ago?' our honest answer would have been, materially yes, morally no."[1] Myers goes on to note that "seventy-six percent of Americans responding to a late 1998 *Washington Post*/Kaiser Foundation/Harvard University poll agreed that the country's 'values and moral beliefs . . . have gotten pretty seriously off on the wrong track'; only 21 percent see them as 'generally going in the right direction.'"[2] These claims are borne out by a number of measures that have tracked the changes over time. Robert Putnam's *Bowling Alone* demonstrates convincingly that over the past, roughly, forty years, a marked reduction in social connectedness and civic-mindedness has occurred. Putnam frames his study in terms of the decline of "social capital," which "refers to connections among individuals — social networks and the norms of reciprocity and trustworthiness that arise from them."[3] Fewer Americans than in the past participate in social groupings, whether bowling leagues, political parties, or religious organizations, even though the participation level of older generations has remained constant. Robert Bellah expresses incisively this decline of social capital across generations, stating that, "Loyalty to others is not high on the agenda of most younger Americans, who can, not entirely accurately, be caricatured as sitting alone at their computers calculating how to maximize their self-interest."[4]

In sum, the nation appears to be on a downward spiral, plummeting toward social and moral bankruptcy, despite its relative economic affluence. While we no longer face societal problems such as child labor, legal segregation, and rampant disease, we also experience greater numbers of crime, divorce, depression, suicide, cohabitation, and children born out of wedlock than in the past.[5] It is a time of "radical individualism," a time of seemingly unlimited freedom to do as one chooses without counting the cost to others. In *The Real American Dream*, Andrew Delbanco frames this loss of social capital in terms of a historical movement away from community values and a concern for others and toward individualism and self-concern. He describes three eras, each shaped by a dominant idea or sustaining narrative: for the Puritans, God; from the Revolutionary War through the Great Society of the 1960s, Nation; and finally, in the current era, Self. It is a story of diminution, for what "Christianity and democracy share is the idea that to live in a purely instrumental relation with other human beings, to exploit and then discard them, is to give in entirely to the predatory instinct and to leave unmet the need for fellowship and reciprocity."[6] The self knows no such maxim.

Bellah amplifies Delbanco's basic premise, suggesting that all three of these dominant ideas have been present in America since the outset, though the "degree of dominance" has varied over time. For Bellah, the key is that, while we no longer confuse the nation with God, as in Ronald Reagan's "shining city on the hill" metaphor, we now confuse the self with God.[7] He notes that piety in the form of "Jesus is my personal Lord and Savior" tends to have a privatizing effect. Emphasizing personal relationship, or "Jesus-and-me piety," the conviction of having Jesus dwelling in one's heart begins an inward spiral in which "the individual [becomes] the preeminent being in the universe."[8] Luther's definition of sin as the *cor curvum in se*, the heart turned in upon itself, comes to mind. Indeed, American society is increasingly focused on individual gain, such that participation in groups is about "what one will get out of participating" and, further, because American individualism is linked to economic individualism, the "only standard is money, and the only thing more sacred than money is more money."[9] Yet in spite of our growing economic individualism and affluence as a society, the statistics also seem to bear out the long-held maxim that money cannot buy happiness or, in the present age, civility and community.

The Role of Christian Faith

As American society appears dangerously threadbare and the public square seemingly lacks moral restraint, Christian circles call for a new commitment or a return to the good old-fashioned values of the church. Indeed, Myers's study would support the notion that religion does exert a restraining influence on behavior: People of faith are "more honest and law abiding and less hedonistic."[10] Religion and faith can and do have a beneficial effect on behavior. Moreover, people of faith are more likely to express compassion and altruism and champion social reform. Yet despite this suggested relationship between faith and morality, Myers is also careful to point out that "religion hardly provides immunity from greed, lust, and bigotry. Examples come easily to mind of faith and *dis*honorable character...."[11]

We need not look far to find evidence of this latter claim. Televangelists prey on the poor, asking them to mail in their hard-earned cash to fund the corporate jet in return for a prayer and a pamphlet. In Texas, Sunday football supplants worship, as pastors hold services before "God's team" kicks off. In Southern California, churchgoers stop at the mall on their way home from Sunday services; the children do battle in the video arcade while the parents make purchases to fill their castle with shiny new armor. In suburban Georgia, the Christian pastor refuses to let the local rabbi fill the pulpit of the Methodist Church during a high school baccalaureate service, claiming it would "be against everything the church stands for." In the Midwest, a conservative Christian group protests at an abortion clinic, and a clinic worker is killed in the name of Jesus Christ. Countless Christians abandon worship altogether because they no longer "get anything out of it"; the sermon is a bore and the music is old and worn. Besides, they can seek and find God on their own. As a recent survey puts it, "people have God within them, so churches aren't really necessary."[12]

Thus, while the Christian character is called into question, mainline Protestant churches struggle against a decline in membership, aging flocks, and empty pulpits. Less than 7 percent of the clergy in mainline denominations are under the age of thirty-five.[13] Mega-churches and even Protestant denominations themselves equate the presence of the Holy Spirit with raw numbers. Like most things American, bigger is better. No matter if those members attend worship services. It is an "all-you-can-eat" mentality in which quality is secondary to self-indulgence, even gluttony. Accountability and service to God and others and the shared intimacy of life together are discarded for the sake of a personal spiritual high. Small rural churches die a slow death because of economic hardship, urban migration, and a graying population. When decline appears, we respond with desperate measures or seek new methods to revitalize our congregations.

Heuristic Models of the Church

In the struggle against this decline, the responses of the Protestant churches tend to cluster into two basic models of life together. These models are intended to be heuristic, suggestive of the problems complicating the life of faith in today's Christian churches, though local churches exist along a spectrum between these two extremes. On the one extreme is the consumerist model, in which the church becomes a commodity and its "services" are consumer-driven. It is a meeting place, a social club, a business network, a daycare center, a source of intellectual stimulation. The church as commodity is a place where members are offered services, which bring them into the fold, but little formation in the faith follows, other than what the individual might choose to pursue. Church membership is considered the mark of discipleship. These churches become the breeding ground of nominal Christians who are given the freedom in Christ to do as they please, to worship as they see fit, to live the good life of prosperity and happiness in the world, to take as their mantra: "God is good all the time. All the time God is good." This is the "postmodern" church in which freedom and pragmatism become paramount; relativism lurks just beyond the stained-glass windows as the key to strong membership rests in giving the consumer what he or she demands. Entertainment and a smorgasbord of programs and services are primary.

At the other extreme are the churches that serve as the locus of moralism. This is the model of the church as regulator of behavior. Religious faith becomes a list of "thou shalls" and "thou shall nots"; membership is premised upon proving oneself dutifully obedient to the commands of God as handed down by the church leadership. Conformity and straightforward answers are primary. This is the church of that old-time religion in which a moral code becomes paramount and absolutism seats itself in the chair beside the pulpit, keeping careful watch over the flock, issuing warnings to steer clear of the world and its evils.

Either version of the Christian life together is partial, incomplete, and lacking in meaning, depth, and vitality. Law and gospel, obedience and freedom are companions on the road of faith, but increasingly the story of the Christian faith appears as a well-worn tale, a tale of two cities: the way of consumerism, which downplays moral choices and a common life of discipleship in favor of cultural acceptability, or the way of legalism, which makes morality authoritative, downplays individual discernment, and stresses a "countercultural" attitude. Christians and non-Christians alike begin to question whether the story has any truth-bearing capacity and spiritual depth, or if, in fact, it is simply a story emerging from the human imagination, lacking historical fact and subject to ongoing embellishment as it passes from generation to generation. The more the story is told, the more fictitious it becomes, until any semblance of truth is buried and cold. When all is said and done, it is just a story that enables us to choose our way in the world, to be our own God or to let someone else be our God. It is a story not unlike any other story read and told.

This decline of the meaning, depth, and vitality of the Christian faith in the contemporary age has led Americans to seek spirituality in places other than more traditionally organized institutional settings. In many ways, religion has become increasingly privatized or individualistic, even as the traditional distinction between public and private continues to blur. For example, home churches are on the rise. A recent study estimated there are as many as sixteen hundred house churches dotting the American landscape.[14] Television talk show hosts promote the personal spiritual journey and recommend different ways of connecting with and developing one's spirit — all of which can be done without ever rising from the comfort of one's sofa. New-age spirituality offers a host of unusual paths that "seekers" eagerly explore, as if sampling food in a trendy new bistro. Other religions attract disillusioned Christians who find the alternative beliefs and practices convey a power and mystery lacking in the contemporary Protestant tradition. Indeed, the institutional Protestant church appears frayed at the edges; the threads are worn to the point of breaking. Perhaps it is time for Protestantism to return to its origins, to be broken open and re-formed. Maybe Robert Bellah is correct in his assessment that "the Reformation was . . . a necessary movement in the spiritual history of humanity, although . . . ultimately it needs to be transcended."[15]

In light of the reality of Christian life today, the vision of the church as the moral foundation of or a transforming social presence in American society grows dim. It is doubtful whether Christians are any more moral than their secular or non-Christian counterparts; it is unlikely that the church can exert a lasting influence on people who see themselves as discrete individuals in the pursuit of material happiness. We are left with the uncomfortable situation of a society whose moral fabric is frayed and a church whose moral virtue seems equally tenuous, no matter how vigorously it is proclaimed or how deliberately downplayed. Our social capital is running dangerously low, inside the church and beyond.

While Myers renews the "can we be good without God?" debate and asks whether, in the absence of faith, we can be good in today's materially prosperous society — even in times when we experience economic downturns — this supposed relationship between God and goodness has been pondered and debated throughout the ages and across changing cultural climates. Today, the question takes on a new twist. We need to recognize that, before we can address the question of our goodness, we must ask the "we" question, the question of our life together within and beyond the church. To do that, we must ask the question of God. In the aftermath of the twentieth century and its unprecedented levels of violence and destruction and equally unprecedented levels of prosperity, we are led to question again whether or not there is any relationship between the good that we seek as human beings and our belief in God. Empirical studies and various assessment methods can only clarify who we are as human beings and North Americans; they cannot tell us who God is. Try as we might, we cannot answer the "God and goodness" question on the basis of statistical measures and anecdotal evidence, even though such data may at times bear witness to a relationship between goodness and belief in God and can further our understanding in certain ways.

From a Christian perspective, which begins with the assumption of faith in the living God, any answer must acknowledge that, by nature, human beings are subject to the power of individual and collective sin; we are not whom we choose and want to be, and we cannot do the good we seek without the power and presence of God. To address the seeming lack of morality in contemporary society, we must first understand that goodness is not a matter of morality only, though moral integrity is a dimension of goodness. The goodness that emerges from genuine relationship to God is also, in its essence, a matter of spiritual integrity. Simply put, it is not a matter of whether God is with us, but whether we respond to God. If we are to contribute meaningfully to strengthening the social fabric of American life and reweaving the rich tapestry of the Christian church, we must begin by reclaiming the spiritual depth of life together. In other words, we must renew the ties, reach out for the lifelines, that connect us to God and others.

HUMAN NATURE AND THE "STATES" OF THE CHURCH

The Social Contract State

In contemporary terms, both the consumerist and regulatory models of the church neglect the fullness of the human condition and the reality of life in God. These models of the church might be viewed as "states" of the church, given that they resemble basic theories of governance. From this perspective of states, we can better discern how the churches are premised upon partial understandings of human nature. John Locke's social contract theory in *A Treatise on Government* provides insight into those churches that emphasize the parishioner as consumer and the church as a commodity or service provider. Suggesting that human nature is basically good, we choose to join together on the basis of the shared common good. We will all be better and receive certain individual benefits as a result of mutuality and respect for one other. Authority resides in the people as a whole, who have entered into the contract, and a spirit of optimism reigns.

Churches that fit this social contract theory often emphasize the love of God and the gospel of prosperity, but give little attention to either the human condition of sin, suffering, and evil or the Christian virtues of faith and hope. The members, as consumers who enter into a contract together, respond to preaching and teaching drawn from motivational techniques and popular psychology laced with a healthy dose of grace. In a society of virtually unlimited choices and increasing wealth, those who join the church prefer not to hear a message that suggests they, too, might be part of the problem. Rather, they seek a message that offers personal fulfillment in the present. They want to be self-actualized, whole people; they come to church to make their lives better in tangible, measurable ways. They try to insulate themselves from the suffering that is all too real for so many people across the earth. Sin and evil are deemed societal forces, controlled as much as possible by Christians' willingness to join together in the spirit of Christian community, acting primarily by giving money and taking occasional mission trips to help the needy.

The Regulatory State

At the other end of the spectrum, the church in its regulatory state concerns itself with personal sin and salvation. Thomas Hobbes's *Leviathan* provides insight into this approach. Life is "short, brutish, and nasty," and we need a strong central authority to protect us from one another. Taking a pessimistic view of human nature, we are thought to be weak and in danger, but in transferring our autonomy to the sovereign, his rules and power preserve our lives. In this state of the church as centralized power, faith in Jesus Christ is central, and obedience to church leadership is essential. Clear rules and regulations enable the members to live in safety and peace. Suffering is often equated with sin: if bad things happen, the cause is sin — breaking the rules — which requires the individual to repent or face the consequences of life apart from the sovereign. Sin is thus the mark of the disobedient life; if people simply follow the rules of the Bible, they can avoid, in large measure, the tendency to sin. Conversely, those who prosper are being blessed by God because they act and pray rightly. Simply stated, sinners refuse to abide by the scriptural imperatives; saints abide by the commandments of the Lord as taught by the church. The proclaimed message is that of obedience to Christ's law, for we are individual sinners who need only behave as Jesus has taught us to do, who need only repent and be saved in him once and for all time. We need only have Jesus in our hearts. Thus, the road to heaven is paved with saving faith, one person at a time; the virtues of hope and love are important to the community, but they are secondary concerns.

In sum, the social contract state of the church holds an optimistic view of human nature and focuses on self-improvement provided by the collective body. Liberal theologies and churches fit this model well. The centralized authority state of the church holds a pessimistic view of human nature and focuses on self-preservation as individuals. Neoorthodox theologies and more traditional churches can be seen to approximate this model. In both cases, we find that considering the states of the church and their views of life together provides us with increased clarity about human nature, but it cannot deepen our understanding of God. As we apply political philosophy to the church as organization or institution, we discover that such approaches can be ventured only from the human perspective, the perspective of our "broken-offness" from the reality of God. In other words, we cannot understand the deeper reality of the church as spiritual community by means of rationality, science, demographics, opinion polls, sociology, political philosophy, rules, regulations, or church law.

Examining the churches as states helps to illuminate the limitations of our models and theories of the church. In the social contract state of the church, the community bases its life together on data, consumer trends, techniques, methods, quantitative measures, reason, and empiricism. As thinking people, we choose those conclusions — and that church — which best fit our understanding of the facts and our needs. In a sense, the social contract church operates on the descriptive, historical, Enlightenment level in which the intellectual pursuit of scientific knowledge, measurable progress, and reasonable proof become important tenets. Once we know the facts, we can live an even better life. The centralized authority state of the church operates on the moral, behavioral, and in some ways, pre-Enlightenment level, in which regulating our actions becomes the key factor in Christian life together. Once we know the rules, we can live a good life by conforming to them and urging others to do the same.

In these states of life together, the reality of life in God or the spiritual level is neglected under the assumption that rationality or morality is sufficient to bring us to the fullness of life in God, or perhaps, considering the sociological analysis that opened this chapter, sufficient to bring us to the fullness of ourselves. Indeed, in today's churches, we might suggest the unmediated presence of God in Christ in the Holy Spirit has been distorted, to some extent, by autonomous rationality and heteronomous moralism, but undoubtedly by the bloated specter of the individual. This notion of the states of the church demonstrates how we choose and, indeed, must choose to create authorities and structures to govern our lives together and with God. Without structures, communal life cannot exist, and without communal life, the Christian way is impossible. However, any such theories about the church cannot manifest the reality of the spiritual life, the reality of God with and among us. The church as institution, social group, state, or whatever analytical model we might draw upon remains a human creation, no different from any other human institution and the surrounding culture, if isolated from the universal gifts of the Spirit of grace — faith, hope, and love — which bind human actuality to that spiritual reality. If we seek to grasp better the spiritual reality that alone can bring the fullness of life into our humanly constructed forms of the church, we must deepen our understanding of the human condition.

The Human Condition: Inherently Good or Defective?

The question of whether human nature is essentially good or evil is misleading theologically. The human creature is a mixture of both, arising out of the *imago Dei* and the condition of sin. Acknowledging the inherent goodness of human life is a necessary step toward renewing the ties that bind us as followers of Christ. Acknowledging the reality and depth of sin as a part of the human condition (in a concrete and a universal sense, applicable to each in particular ways and to all in the sense of its inevitability) is an equally necessary step toward renewing those ties.

Although at different times in the history of Christianity, theologians and believers have struggled against the "flesh" and upheld the need to mortify its passions, the basic fact that we are human beings, created in bodies and with limits, is not, in and of itself, a problem. In the beginning, as the first creation story proclaims, God created the man and the woman in the divine image (Gen. 1:27), and the human form was deemed to be very good, for everything God made was very good (Gen. 1:31). The Genesis narratives reveal that we were created like God in certain ways, with certain capacities. We have capacities beyond those possessed by or given to other creatures, especially free will or the freedom to choose our way of being in the world. We have been given gifts of moral accountability, consciousness, and choice — though the reality of sin diminishes our original giftedness and goodness. These capacities in no way privilege the human creature, but indicate difference and responsibility. Being a human being in a physical body was deemed to be a very good work of a loving God, enabling good and loving work to be done in and through that body and life. Thus, our creatureliness, embodied form, and finitude are not the fundamental problems of existence. We were created as a reflection of the glory of God, in order to glorify God through our lives and our bodies, and much about the human body is to be celebrated.

Yet something about our existence is undeniably problematic. Something about our existence leads us to ponder the meaning and mystery of life as we know it and to rail against its injustices and sorrows. Anyone who has experienced the loss of a loved one, suffered through a terrible illness, or walked amid the desperate poverty in which so many of God's children live recognizes in a profound way that sooner or later each of us will ask what it means to be a human being in this world. Sooner or later each of us will be forced to accept that we are subject to decay and death, as well as the unrelenting unfairness and inequality of life in its quantity, quality, beauty, justice, and dignity. At other moments, we are enveloped in the depths of loneliness. No matter how close we may be to our families or how many good friends we may have, we continue to yearn for a deeper, more tangible, more permanent connectedness. We yearn for lasting bonds and absolutely reliable support systems. Moreover, the less we have materially, the more important the human connection becomes and the more debilitating its loss. The older we grow, the more we are forced to contemplate and confront our own death and what it means to leave behind this body, earth, and life as we know them. Simply living in the world puts us in touch with the root problem, the problem of our existence, the problem of inching toward death with each breath that we take. Life itself forces us to consider the reality of being human in its giftedness, incompleteness, and transitoriness.

From this viewpoint of the benevolent and tragic dimensions of human nature, it becomes clear that both states of the church fail to deal adequately with the presence of sin. If human nature is fundamentally good, sin is narrowed to a condition largely controlled by our collective efforts as we focus on God's unending love for us and the possibilities for living the good life. If, on the other hand, human nature is fundamentally flawed, sin becomes a condition regulated and kept in check by faithful obedience to an identifiable set of God's rules. Sin, however little or much we may talk about it in our churches, is a pervasive reality that suggests a great deal about who we are as human beings created to live a good life, but unable to do so by our own efforts.

Sin, in its most basic sense, is rejecting or denying God's presence through the exercise of our human capacities. While it is often referred to as "turning away from God," sin is a far more decisive act than merely turning our backs on God. First, sin as the rejection or denial of God's presence through the exercise of our human capacities suggests that God is omnipresent. God's grace — the love and undeserved favor of God toward us, which enables relationships to flourish — surrounds us and whispers to us at every step we take, whether we are aware of that love or not. God's grace calls to us like a lover upon seeing the beloved. There is never a moment of our existence in which God is not present to and with us. Even in the midst of the terrorist events of September 2001, an overflowing abundance of God's grace was evident despite our usual proclivity toward self-fulfillment: expressions of love voiced by victims in their final moments, lines curling around blocks as people waited to donate blood, firefighters and police officers endangering their own lives to help others escape, rescue workers appearing from every corner of the country needing "to do something." God's grace overflowed in radically visible and present ways.

Yet despite the ubiquity of grace, we have the capacity to close off and reject or deny God's gracious presence. To confirm this capacity, we need only to consider the looting that took place in the stores beneath the ruins of the World Trade Center or the people who made false claims to capitalize financially on the donations for those who suffered losses in the tragedy. In the midst of overwhelming and deeply disturbing violence and death, some Americans felt compelled to seek their own gain, to take what they could while others were focused on rescue and recovery efforts. This capacity to reject God's grace, which often begins with the exercise of reason and ends in a self-justifying choice, leads to a second dimension of sin: freely choosing to act in ways other than those that God would have us choose. We conclude that God's way is not in our best interest and choose to follow a path of our own making and our own taking. Such a path leads us away from God and toward the self.

Historically, the Christian tradition has focused on the problem of individual sin, but in more recent years, liberation theologians have introduced the important insight that communal forms of sin are equally real and destructive of lives — an insight arising precisely at a time when social capital began to decline. Structural and institutional sin diminishes freedom and genuine choice for countless people. Social, political, military, and economic structures and institutions create and sustain unjust and dehumanizing conditions in which we participate by varying degrees and with varying intentionality. Failure to repent of our complicity in systemic oppression through ignorance, denial, feigned impotence, laziness, or apathy leads us to reject God's presence through the misuse or misdirection of our capacities. In many ways, we must recognize how the collective sin of the United States over decades, even centuries, may have contributed to the hatred felt by citizens of other nations toward the United States, even though genuine acts of goodness and aid have also been our collective legacy. While acknowledging our collective sin does not justify terrorist responses, we cannot ignore the ways in which our domestic, foreign, and trade or business policies impact the lives of persons both within and outside the boundaries of the United States. The sin — whether individual or collective — is ours, and we are accountable to God and others for it. Thus, sin is a reality that grips us as individuals and as communities of various sizes, shapes, and purposes.

There is yet more to the condition of sin, however, for sin is not simply the choice to reject or deny God's love. Indeed, there is a power, a force, a magnetism wielded by sin that holds us captive and prevents us from doing the good we would choose to do. On the communal or macro level, forms of collective sin and social power wielded by unjust structures and institutions limit the possibilities and well-being of large numbers of people. Freedom of choice and access to power, education, and goods are not equally distributed. On the individual or micro level, sin exerts a power over our lives. As Paul wrote to the Romans, "For I do not do the good I want, but the evil I do not want is what I do. Now if I do what I do not want, it is no longer I that do it, but sin that dwells within me" (Rom. 7:19–20). While our post-Enlightenment sensibilities tend to scoff at the notion of sin as a power that exerts a very real influence upon us, we need not look far to see that our original goodness is tarnished or sullied. Parents know well the experience of giving birth to an infant and watching its sweet, gentle ways transition into the time we have aptly named "the terrible twos." While there is a wonderful side to the growing independence of a child, there is also the recognition that at some point, by our very nature, we resist doing what is good. Those same parents know well the child who has tried so hard to be helpful and, instead, has created more of a mess. All of us regret deeply the times we have hurt others or failed to render help, but could not explain why. We may be capable of rationalizing and finding some justification for our action or inaction, but in a very basic sense, we realize we are struggling against something beyond our ability to control and eliminate. In a similar manner, on the systemic level, we acknowledge that we are caught up in systems not of our making or choosing as individuals, yet we cannot entirely extricate ourselves from them — nor, at times, do we wish to fully extricate ourselves, despite recognizing the harm that they do to others and, possibly, to ourselves. It is ironic that as our understanding of collective forms of sin began to grow, our participation in group activities where we might seek to alter unjust and dehumanizing institutions plummeted. In spite of our decreased activism or agency, the fact remains that we can and must attempt to do what is right; that is our responsibility as human beings. We can and will fail; that is our condition as human beings.

If we turn to the second creation story in Genesis 2:4b–3:24, we find that in the beginning human beings were bound to God in an intimate relationship. God was not a critical principle, a giver of rules, or an unmoved mover, but a constant unmediated presence who walked with the human creatures in the garden. In our contemporary era, we cannot fathom a life lived in the fullness of relationship to God and others, but this creation story suggests the first people knew God in terms of relationship, and they knew nothing but this unmediated presence. They knew only the fullness of relationship. Then came the break. We, as God's human creatures, excused ourselves and our actions from the presence of God. In dismissing ourselves, we broke the ties, the lifelines, that connected us to God and one another. We chose to reject that intimate bond. We failed to be in conversation with God, the ever-present Word, and let our reasoning be our guide. Although there was only one law given, we could not adhere to this one, single moral directive. Instead, we took life into our own hands;

we exchanged words without including the Word that was present in the beginning; and as a result, we were no longer bound to the Word of Life, but forced to govern our lives without the unity and unmediated presence that we enjoyed in the beginning.

Only then did commandment enter our world as prohibition, as "other," standing against us, rather than with us, dividing us and showing us our inability to live life as it was intended to be lived. In our broken-offness from God and one another, otherness as division, rather than unity and relationship, entered into our awareness and our world. Today, we experience this as brokenness. Our individual and social relationships are broken in many and varied ways. By excusing ourselves from God's presence, we removed ourselves from the ultimate good and from the essence of relationality. Only the dingy image of God's goodness remains within us as a constant reminder of the possible; not eradicated, but diminished. Now, try as we might to do the good, we cannot sustain our efforts. Try as we might — and we must try — to fix ourselves, our institutions, our world, we can only manage modest improvements and, sometimes, further erosion. No matter how hard we try, we must acknowledge we cannot save ourselves from ourselves or the injustices of others. No amount of fame, fortune, prestige, power, beauty, or privilege saves us from ourselves or the injustices of the world. Such things do not save a single human being from decay and death. Without God's unmediated presence, we are unable to live in that state of unbroken connectedness to God and others for which we long. In the end, even straining to follow God's will for our lives leads, at best, to uncertainty and, at worst, to sheer failure and regret. Although in a historical sense, we cannot grasp the actual details of this initial break from God's unmediated presence, we can grasp its meaning for our lives as it enables us to envision sin as a condition that permeates our lives. To be free from all sin is not within our control, even though to be less prone to sin is our calling.

This understanding of sin leads to a fundamental paradox of the Christian faith: We can never know with absolute certainty whether we are following God's way or justifying our own selfish choices by talking only to ourselves. In other words, absolute knowledge of God's will and way remains beyond our grasp, for in this life we see in a mirror, dimly (1 Cor. 13:12). Perhaps, if we are not cautious, when we gaze into that glass, we see only ourselves. Even our best intentions, over time, may prove to be contrary to God's will. Even our best intentions may prove to be self-motivated. Thomas Merton expressed well this situation in a simple prayer:

> My Lord God, I have no idea where I am going. I do not see the road ahead of me. I cannot know for certain where it will end. Nor do I really know myself, and the fact that I think I am following your will does not mean that I am actually doing so. But I believe that the desire to please you does in fact please you. And I hope I have that desire in all that I am doing. I hope that I will never do anything apart from that desire. And I know that if I do this you will lead me by the right road, though I may know nothing about it.[16]

God's will for our lives is a constant process of discernment and growing in wisdom, through our participation in the reality of God in Christ in the Holy Spirit. It involves errors in judgment and learning to discern better what God would have us do, and this process occurs on both the individual and communal levels. We might say that we live in an uncertain certainty, as we trust that God's way is in our best interest, but are confronted with the uncertainty of choosing our life moment by moment, recognizing that individual and collective sin continues to wreak havoc upon our world. We need others to serve as companions on the journey of faith and discernment, encouraging us and holding us accountable. We need God's unmediated presence in the body of Christ, building us up and knitting us together. We need to acknowledge who we are and what we are not; only then may we begin to renew the ties that bind us to God, one another, and the whole web of creation.

BOUND TOGETHER
IN FAITH, HOPE, AND LOVE

Having now argued that the states of the church are human arrangements founded on partial and incomplete understandings of the human condition and that God's love and grace are ever present, whether or not we recognize or accept them, we are left with a picture of the church as a human activity in need of the unmediated presence of God. It is the spiritual dimension, the unmediated presence of God, which forms the church in its most genuine or essential sense. The spiritual dimension might best be described, by means of the Pauline metaphor of the body of Christ, as inescapable, constant, radical relationality. In Christ and through the Holy Spirit, the church as the body of Christ exists as the unmediated presence of God in the world today. In Christ, as the body of Christ, we now participate directly, by means of the Holy Spirit, in God's presence, and we are bound to one another in ways that our pragmatic, empirically oriented minds can scarcely grasp. In God in Christ in the Holy Spirit, we are bound to the whole of creation and placed into a position of responsibility toward all. We can deny and reject our relationality and responsibility, but they remain present and gnaw at the edges of our consciousness.

Too often we speak of the spiritual life, God's presence, or the reality of the body of Christ as if they were concepts or metaphors only. We speak as if God is a "critical principle," which we must bracket out of our theological reflection in order to speak intelligibly to the culture. We speak as if the "grammar of faith" is only a language that enables us to order our human lives according to certain understandings, conventions, and practices. We speak as if God's realm on earth is a rulebook and a checklist. We speak as if the social, economic, and political order or our culture is the problem to be solved. Entangled in our own words and ideas, we forget that God IS. God is the I AM of Exodus 3:14. Despite our inability to fully grasp or convey this reality, we who call ourselves followers of Christ know at the deepest level that God IS. To paraphrase Paul Tillich, God is the really real.

God is the life that we seek to embrace, the community for which we yearn, the world as it should be, the fullness of life for the whole of creation.

Despite our intellectual, psychological, and scientific difficulties with God as a *living* God (in an ontotheological sense), the state of being in God, belonging to the body of Christ is a reality. While the evidence is intangible and the state of being in God in Christ in the Holy Spirit can only be realized by faith, it is nonetheless real. It is neither a figment of our imaginations nor the projections of human wishes and desires; life in God is reality, if we open ourselves to receive and cultivate it in our daily lives. While we continue to live as persons yearning for permanent connectedness and for meaning in a world filled with suffering and death, God's unmediated presence is a reality given to us in Christ and through the Holy Spirit as members of the body of Christ. Specifically, the ties that connect us to God and one another — whether we are in a social contract state, a centralized authority state, or some hybrid version of the church — are the universal spiritual gifts of faith, hope, and love, otherwise known as the theological virtues. We must open ourselves to accept them and let them infuse our life and action in the world.

We might think of *these three* — faith, hope, and love — as intertwined threads that connect us to God like an umbilical cord, unseen yet very real, providing us with nourishment and enabling us to grow to maturity and to be active, concerned citizens of both the city of God and of humanity. Faith accepts that God's way is in our best interest, despite "evidence" or societal pressures to the contrary. Faith is the entryway to the journey, which must be sustained over a lifetime. Hope is the momentum and the compass for the journey in God; it keeps us traveling toward home, waiting and working in this world and its woes, remaining open to new possibilities for life. Love is both the source of our life and the destination we seek as it seeks us. Love is a destination that we glimpse, a reality in which we participate, and a realm to which we contribute along the way, and it becomes more pronounced the more we open ourselves to the life of God with and among us. These three interconnected, interwoven gifts of God form the Christ-character in us, the growing reflection of God's glory and realm among us, and tether us to the unmediated presence of God and to others in the body of Christ. The Christ-character is never an individual condition only, but it is inescapably communal and relational. We cannot grow into the likeness of Christ or be a Christ for others, to use Dietrich Bonhoeffer's phrase, unless we are in responsible relationship to others.

Thus, as we recognize that the church as institution is not so cleanly differentiated from the political state as institution, and that the church as institution manifests and actualizes itself in various forms, we begin to see that the shape of life in God is not a pattern of separate spheres or circles on a Venn diagram, such that we are either inside or outside the spiritual life. Rather, the shape of life in God is more akin to a fabric. Christians and people of other religious faiths, church and state, those who believe in the inherent goodness of human nature and those who believe in its inherent evilness, all human beings are woven together in the fabric of life. We cannot extricate ourselves from the fabric of this created world or from God's constant presence, even as we may reject or deny it. Apart from God, there can be history, as we interpret the course of human events. Apart from God, there can be culture, as we create value systems and ways of organizing our lives and societies. Apart from God, there can be moral imperatives and laws that seek to control our behavior. But apart from God, there cannot be the deepest reality of the spiritual life or the Christian journey, the reality of who we are created to be and whom we yearn to become. Apart from God and the threads of faith, hope, and love, we are left to our own devices and limited choices under the guise of complete freedom. These three are the ties that bind us to God and others; they form the umbilical cord that nourishes us and enables us to grow in God and into the character of Christ as responsible, radical relationality.

In the pages that follow, we begin to recover the theological virtues as a central doctrine in the Christian life and understanding. In chapter 2, we examine the nature of myth and argue that the myths of scripture are crucial to our participation in God. Then, we explore the origins of the notion of virtue in Plato and Aristotle, and we trace, briefly, the development of the Christian doctrine of the theological virtues in the writings of Augustine and Aquinas, as a means of providing a backdrop to our more constructive chapters. Chapters 3, 4, and 5 focus on each of the three virtues, beginning with faith in God in contrast to four contemporary distortions of "faith," turning to hope in contrast to the face of contemporary hopelessness, and arriving at love as the source and destination of the Christian journey. The epilogue weaves together these ties to demonstrate that they are inseparable and essential beliefs and practices of the Christian journey. Faith, hope, and love — as the ties that bind us to God and others — are the means by which we participate in God in the present. Together they energize and empower the spiritual journey and form the Christ-character in individuals and communities of faith. They are inherently relational and place us into relationship with God and one another, though what we do with those relationships remains open. As such, the theological virtues can have an energizing, empowering, and transforming effect on the larger social fabric within which we live and practice our faith, hope, and love. We can make a significant difference in this world, but not without faith, hope, and love, these three, which connect us to God and God's grace.

Chapter Two

THESE THREE
IN HISTORICAL PERSPECTIVE

In the previous chapter we argued that our contemporary Protestant churches need to reclaim and rekindle the spiritual dimension of life together in a deeper and richer sense. This statement requires a bit of qualification and clarification. When we seek to renew the spiritual dimension or the reality of intimacy with the living God, we are in no way suggesting that the spiritual realm is somehow absent from this world. To the contrary, we are surrounded by and embedded in the spiritual, but our capacity to fully receive and participate in the reality of God with and among us is diminished or underdeveloped. Our spiritual senses — the eyes, ears, noses, tongues, and skin of faith that enable us to recognize and experience the presence of the living God with and among us — have grown dull and lethargic through neglect.[1] To begin our recovery of these three, we explore, first, the importance of the mythic world of the Scriptures and, second, the rise of the theological virtues in Greek and Christian thought.

THE MYTHIC WORLD OF SCRIPTURE

The Scriptures as "Myths"

The dulling of our spiritual senses is a phenomenon whose roots reach back into the Enlightenment and the long process in which reason, the autonomous individual, and the scientific mind-set grew to characterize modernity. While the Enlightenment agenda contributed to human flourishing by dismantling the unquestioned authority of those in power and making viable the priesthood of all believers, it also led to discrediting, deconstructing, and dismissing "myth" and the narrative world of scripture, the stories of faith. Theologian Edward Farley has referred to this phenomenon, the loss of the mythical and symbolic aspects of life in North America, as the "disenchantment" of symbols or words of power. Farley defines "deep symbols" as "the values by which a community understands itself, from which it takes its aims, and to which it appeals as canons of cultural criticism. To grow up in a community is to have one's consciousness shaped by these symbols."[2] Although he focuses on so-called words of power such as obligation, the real, and hope — rather than the myths and stories of the Scriptures — Farley's point bears consideration because it highlights our diminished capacity for mystery. We no longer comprehend how "finite reality participates in sacred power, the infinite creativity."[3] In other words, our worldview and enculturation are such that we are less apt to approach the reality of mystery and the sacred with a sense of awe and acceptance; instead, we tend to believe that reality lies in the realm of what can be empirically verified. "Seeing is believing" has become our watchword.

As this dilemma grew to its fullness in the modern period, various attempts at reconciling the mythic world of scripture with the enlightened world of modernity emerged. Rudolf Bultmann's project of "demythologizing" and Paul Tillich's desire to "remythologize" scripture in the language of the day epitomized the modern approach. These and other scholars called into question the biblical stories and the language of faith as products of a more primitive worldview, which the mature West had outgrown. As a result, they sought to scrape away the unsophisticated human elements of the story and to arrive at the kernel of truth, as if extracting gold ore from rock, discarding the mythical elements as dross. For Tillich, the subsequent move involved reconceptualizing those truths in modern terms, especially using the language of depth psychology so prominent in his time. Thus, God became the "Ground of Being" and, as we see in chapter 4, hope became "the courage to be." Today, we continue to draw upon these insights, as we make meaningful the stories and narratives of scripture in contemporary terms. Yet we also realize that the search for "the" truth of each text is, at heart, an attempt to reduce and limit God's Word to what can be understood by human beings.

If we consult a dictionary, we find that by definition a myth is fictitious; it does not have any basis in fact or reality. We might say, there is no proof, no way to verify that the story happened precisely as written or told. Yet, in practice, myths have a powerful ability to shape our lives in the world, even in present times. Joseph Campbell, the prolific scholar of religions, argued that myths arise from the collective unconscious or the creative imagination and serve to shape the moral order of a given society. Myths help us make sense of our lives and our world; they give us directions for navigating across the landscape of our days on earth. Campbell included the sciences within his concept of myth, because they likewise depend upon the creative imagination for their discoveries, revisions, and ongoing search for knowledge about human life, the world, and the cosmos.[4] We might suggest, then, there is something fundamentally human about this process of searching for and living by our collective narratives. Social and scientific myths, not unlike religious myths, function to shape our understanding and how we enter into life together as societies and as communities of faith. If such myths did not exist, we would become immobilized, lacking guidance for negotiating life on earth.

Yet despite the significance of his insights, Campbell, much like Bultmann and Tillich before him, was a product of modernity and its deeply held assumptions. His idea of myth tends to subjectivize and internalize the mythic world, suggesting, along the lines of Freud or Feuerbach, that myths are essentially projections of our own human longings and desires. However, from the perspective of faith, the stories or narratives of the Scriptures, including both the Hebrew Scriptures and New Testament, are not mythical in this sense of being human projections — that is, as offering only our own deeply held wishes and values or, more correctly, those of our imaginative forbears. Although we long for relationship with the living God, for justice and peace on earth, we do so because we have been loved and known by God first, as a prior condition. We live according to the belief that the reality of God is not a figment of our imagination. As such, the Scriptures express or reveal the alternative reality of God in Christ in the Holy Spirit, and the germ of truth cannot be neatly extracted from the mythic aspects or from the context of human life together before and with God. The Word of God in scripture originates in the mysterious reality beyond our grasp and control.

Accepting that the Scriptures make manifest an alternative reality does not imply, however, that we should thus understand the Bible in a precritical, literal sense, holding that each story occurred exactly as written, flowing directly and without error from God to the hand of a human scribe. In other words, the Bible is not a window to heaven on earth, through which we look and clearly see the reality of God. Indeed, the finitude and fallibility of our human nature remain intertwined with the Word of God in scripture, and the reality of God remains ambiguously present in our words. When the eternal Word becomes historical words, the clarity and unity are diffused and elude our grasp like the cottony seeds of a dandelion blown about by the wind. The stories and myths of scripture retain a truth-bearing quality; nonetheless, we cannot peel away the narrative and expose basic propositional truths that can then be applied to our lives in any and all circumstances. Similarly, the Scriptures should not be viewed simply as historical documents, a window on the past, lacking any power or authority in our contemporary lives and, therefore, requiring us to eliminate those aspects of the texts that historical and literary evidence cannot authenticate. Further, the Scriptures should not be viewed from an existentialist perspective as merely a window into ourselves or, better, a mirror in which I see only myself reflected. Instead, we should recognize that the Scriptures are more akin to home movies where we ask one another about what was happening and why we did certain things, knowing that different participants understand and tell the story differently. Or we might view the Scriptures as a painting or sculpture that we stand in front of, attempting to discern the intent of the creator and what the artwork means to us as we participate in it.

The sacred Scriptures of the Christian faith embody and participate in a power that, in turn, can enable us to embody and participate in an alternative way of approaching our life in the world. They open us to the reality of the living God and enable us to live and move within that reality. Thus, the Bible is not a work of fiction, history, or a rule book; it is more akin to a travel guide that opens us to the life of the Spirit and enables us to see and experience the landscape and recognize how and where the reign of God is breaking into our world. It facilitates our participation in the realm of God, as it opens us to the alternative reality, and we respond in faith, hope, and love.

To be Christian is to enter intentionally and regularly — as well as to enter faithfully, hopefully, and lovingly — into the myths and stories of the Scriptures, to make them our own, and to continue the narrative through our lives and witness in pursuit of justice and peace. For this reason, the Bible remains central to the Christian life. We need to rekindle our relationship with the Word of God in scripture. New Testament scholar Marcus Borg offers one approach. He claims that reading the Bible in our contemporary era warrants a "historical-metaphorical" approach that can bring to light its truth-bearing character. He recognizes that, as a result of the Enlightenment process and the deliteralizing of the Bible, we have become skeptics, uncertain about the reality of the spiritual life. Yet we also sense that stories and myths can be true without being literally true. Thus, Borg suggests that we should understand the Bible as a human response to God that "define[s] who we are in relation to God and who we are as a community and as individuals."[5] Scripture is a "lens," enabling us to see the reality of God, but it is not, in and of itself, that reality. We might suggest that the Bible facilitates a relationship; it invites our participation in the life of God in Christ in the Holy Spirit in the world. The Bible shapes the way we encounter and experience reality as it conveys the activity of God in the past, present, and future by means of metaphor or indirect language that points us to God and says, "God is like...; God is not like...." We read and enter into the Scriptures to glimpse and better understand God and the journey of faith; to reorient our lives in relation to others and the created world; and to be people of faith, who participate in the realm of God breaking into our world.

Myths of Our Contemporary Society

Believing in stories and myths is not as uncommon in our contemporary society as we might initially think. Such myths continue to shape our view of society, though seldom do we seek to strip down these stories and myths to the bare kernel of truth and expose the inadequacies and injustices of our society's mythical world — a point that liberation theologians often make as they illuminate social and institutional structures of sin. We need not look far to see that as an enlightened, postmodern society, myths continue to hold sway in our collective consciousness. A good example is the American myth that "anyone can grow up to be president." In a legal and procedural sense, this statement is true: every child born a citizen of this country has the legal and procedural possibility of growing up to be president. But in practice, it is quite obvious that the statement is far from true. Barriers — erected by our society and institutions — of race, sex, class, religious affiliation, sexual orientation, and education bar the way for the vast majority of Americans to consider, even remotely, a run for the presidency. Even so, when a child is born, the possibility of his or her future in the White House cannot be discounted entirely. It is a myth, an oft-told tale, that bears an element of truth and shapes our understanding of life together in the United States, even though empirical data and facts tend to discredit the claim more than lend credence to it.

Consider the myth, propagated in the modern era and continuing to cling to the American psyche, of progress toward a better world through science and technology. Few would dispute that science and technology have bettered our lives significantly: the treatment and eradication of diseases, the increasing availability of fresh water and food supplies, superior communications via e-mail and cellular phones, and so forth, which enhance the quality and quantity of life, as well as its safety, convenience, and enjoyment. But few people would dispute that such gains have come at a cost: the proliferation of military arms, the growing disparity between rich and poor, the magnitude of human-generated disasters, and the rise of stress-related illnesses are but a few examples. Clearly, science and technology are not the panacea that we once believed them to be, even as they continue to hold out the promise of a better, less troubled future for our society. We continue to turn to science and technology as the answers to our human woes, yet, inevitably, new problems arise along with these "solutions."

A third contemporary myth, exposed by philosopher Alasdair MacIntyre, is the widespread belief in managerial expertise. This myth holds sway over many of our churches, as pastors see themselves as CEOs and statistical data replaces spiritual formation as the measure of "success." Not unlike the precritical belief in God prior to the Enlightenment, MacIntyre contends the uncritical acceptance of the expertise of today's managers and managerial techniques is of mythic proportions: the "concept of managerial effectiveness is...a contemporary moral fiction. The power which is afforded to such managerial experts far exceeds the reality of what a manager can predict and control in the organization or in society."[6] Managers learn and seek to be "scientific," to use numbers and techniques, yet institutions remain riddled with the inconsistencies of human behavior and the randomness inherent in life.

If we accept MacIntyre's premise, that social and institutional behavior is far more random and uncontrollable than we care to admit, then the myth we are perpetuating today is that through these experts our world and lives can be secure, stable, and predictable. We continue to seek certainty rather than ambiguity, order rather than chaos, control rather than randomness. Where once the common belief was that God is in control and all will be well; today it is that a well-degreed manager is in control and all will be well. We thus live our lives according to what the "experts," such as church growth specialists, predict and recommend, even though they, too, admit that many unknown variables can radically alter the direction that our churches, institutions, society, economy, and defense efforts take. Perhaps this myth is even more evident in the wake of numerous corporate accounting and management scandals in which the costs have been borne, not by the experts who have failed to exercise responsible leadership, but by the people who can least afford to bear such losses. Certainly, managers and church leaders with wisdom, careful training, experience, and integrity can make major contributions to the functioning and well-being of our social order and institutions. But managerial expertise is far from being the scientific process and safeguard many assume it to be — perhaps, above all, because we cannot factor out the human element and the unpredictability of life on earth.

Theologically, then, we recognize that, despite our best intentions to provide equal opportunity to the highest office in the land and to use our knowledge to improve human life, we fall short of the mark. A radical break lies between our claimed social order and the reality of our lives, yet we cannot ignore that myths and stories, which are neither completely factual nor completely fictitious, permeate and shape our lives. Myths and the ritual acts that often accompany them are woven into the structures of our lives, our values, and our choices. It is particularly evident that myths and rituals carry and convey us in and through the liminal moments of our existence. The birth of an infant in all its mystery and the silence that shrouds physical death cannot be navigated by means of facts and techniques alone. Noting the number of births per annum or the average life span in a country does nothing to convey the depths of God with us, though such statistics may convey how little we care for others who are struggling for life and well-being. The grandeur of the universe and the infinite complexity of planet Earth are beyond our grasp, even in the most advanced societies, even as scientists point ever more powerful telescopes and satellites toward the heavens and astronauts inhabit temporary homes with stunning views of Earth. Much of our life remains shaped by value-bearing and value-laden myths and stories. These stories, which are common in our contemporary world, convey — as well as conceal — truths about who we are and how we relate to our world and one another.

For Christians, the myths and stories of scripture open us to a particular reality that would otherwise remain hidden or uninhabitable. They often call into question the myths of our society that do not contribute to the flourishing of life for all. As sacred scripture, the stories of the faith reveal deeper truths about a specific aspect of existence: our life with God, one another, and the whole of creation. The Scriptures speak most clearly about life lived in relationship, rather than as self-serving and solitary individuals, and they promote values that, at times, conflict with societal norms. While we may debate the historical veracity of various texts and claims, there remains a spiritual reality at work in and through the biblical narrative, and it is imperative for the life of the church that we learn again and again how to participate in scripture and the spiritual reality it conveys. Myths pervade our lives, whether consciously or not, but the biblical stories enable us to enter into a reality that is otherwise hidden. Rather than dismissing the stories as myths of an earlier generation, we need to regain a sense of imagination and awe as people of God in a world of immense complexity and beauty, a world that we know and experience as tragically and undeniably flawed. It is a world in which the goal of life-giving relationships can be realized and the myths of individualism at the expense of others and the natural world are unmasked. As philosopher Paul Ricoeur has expressed, when we enter into the biblical text, we are changed by our encounter with it and enabled to "return" to the world to live differently. Our eyes are opened to a new way of being in the world. The Bible continues to transform us into people of God and to form the

Christ-character in us, if we are open to having our vision and our steps redirected.

Levels of Interpretation in the Scriptures

When we read the Scriptures, we need to recognize the various levels on which the biblical texts can speak to us. Throughout Christian history, theologians such as Origen, Augustine, Aquinas, and Luther have insisted that multiple levels of interpretation and engagement are evoked by the sacred texts. While a comprehensive treatment of the history of interpretation is beyond the scope of this work, we can simplify the various approaches of these thinkers and point toward three basic or primary ways of reading and responding to the Scriptures: (1) historical-descriptive interpretation, (2) moral-prescriptive interpretation, and (3) spiritual-theological interpretation. One or more of these levels may be at work in a given passage of scripture, and each of the levels builds upon the others to form the deepest sense of the biblical witness.

First, the most direct sense of the text, the historical-descriptive, conveys information about the culture, people, places, languages, and events of the ancient world. For example, in chapter 2 of Luke's Gospel, we are given historical details that set the framework for the birth of Jesus: "In those days a decree went out from Emperor Augustus that all the world should be registered. This was the first registration and was taken while Quirinius was governor of Syria" (2:1–2). In these verses, we find historical information about the governance of Palestine and the ancient census that was taken. From other sources, we can then determine that this occurred in the first decade B.C.E., because Augustus reigned as emperor from 27 B.C.E. to 14 C.E., and that Quirinius was the military leader or governor of Syria at the time. In this way, we are able grasp the historical and descriptive sense of the passage. Our historical consciousness is awakened to another time and place, and our understanding begins to take shape.

The next interpretative layer of scripture is that of the moral or prescriptive dimension. At this level, we become aware of how we should live our lives as people of God, in relationship to others and to our created world. Obvious examples of this would include the Ten Commandments (Exod. 29:1–17 and Deut. 5:6–21) and the Great Commandment to love God and others found in Matthew 22:37–39 and Luke 10:27. But more subtle admonitions to act in certain ways are numerous. For example, in Genesis we are told to be caretakers of the earth, acting in ways that facilitate its well-being. The prophets repeatedly invoke our responsibility toward those who are marginalized in society: the poor, the widow, the orphan, the foreigner. In a similar manner, the invitations Jesus extends to the marginalized and excluded, in both his ministry and his parables, prescribe an inclusive and welcoming attitude toward others, an attitude of hospitality and concern for strangers and those who are different from ourselves, as well as those whom we know and resemble. In the letters of Paul, we find frequent references to how we ought to behave as Christians, including such actions as speaking the truth, doing honest work, sharing with the needy, offering forgiveness, renouncing greed and fornication, pursuing peace with all. If we return to Luke 2:1–2, we might even suggest that the subsequent verses are open to an element of moral-prescriptive interpretation, for Joseph obeys the laws of the empire and travels with Mary to register his household. We might understand this as suggesting that people of faith are to uphold the laws of the land, at least so far as they do not conflict with God's claim upon our lives and world. The moral-prescriptive level of scripture thus offers insights into how we should live in the world and with one another. It tells us something about how to live a good life. We become aware that we are obligated to act in certain ways in the present and in light of the desired future.

Finally, the deepest and most abstract level of interpretation is the spiritual-theological. We might say that this level speaks to us about how to live, not simply a good life, but a godly life, a life in conversation with the deepest level of reality. The spiritual dimension of scripture speaks to us about our relationship with God and the life of faith; it illuminates our calling to be agents of transformation

and justice in the world. If the historical-descriptive sense of the
Scriptures provides us with information, and the moral-prescriptive
sense is geared toward formation, at this level of interpretation, the
Scriptures speak in personal and communal ways that promote transformation in the depths of our being and societies and in the fullness
of the created world.

At the level of spiritual-theological interpretation, much like hearing a sermon, a particular passage may resonate in various ways with
different people and communities, and the interpretation is shaped
by the context in which it is read. Yet there are boundaries to what
is "heard" in a particular passage. An individual interpretation of
scripture at the spiritual-theological level withstands the test of two
criteria that facilitate a diffusion of the power to interpret: (1) the affirmation of the larger Christian community across time, space, and
culture, and (2) the overall tenor or message of the Scriptures such
that no individual passage is held as more important or of greater
weight than the biblical understanding of the journey of faith and
what it means to be a follower of God in Christ in the Holy Spirit
discernable in the broad patterns and teachings. In this life, as finite
people limited by time, space, culture, experience, and knowledge,
we see "in a mirror, dimly." As finite beings, we cannot possess the
full knowledge and understanding of God and the things of God,
such that we must remain in dialogue with the community of believers found in the church universal and with the community of texts
found in the Bible as a whole. While human societies are noted for
marginalizing and oppressing groups of people, the Scriptures form
a common table around which we gather as equals, as children of
God. The Bible is a table at which all are welcome, even if some try
to hoard the Word for personal gain. We are limited in what we can
know and grasp, and we must always be open to the possibility that
our understanding is in error. Indeed, we can learn this sense of the
provisional nature of our understanding from the scientific community, whose hypotheses remain open to revision in light of further
knowledge and "revelation."

The level of spiritual-theological interpretation is the least recognized and most important dimension of the Scriptures for the
Christian journey because at this level our vision is redirected to the
reality of God's reign on earth. Here we find openings to God's way
in the world; we are able to journey through life as people who recognize and participate in God's presence and guidance in the details and
most ordinary moments of our lives. It is not possible, of course, to
offer a definitive example of spiritual-theological interpretation given
that the Scriptures live and breathe on this level. However, illustra-
tions are possible in both concrete and more general expressions. For
example, women reading the Bible together in Latin America have
found themselves opened to a far deeper relationship with Christ, as
they learn about and grow into the gospel message of life and liberation in the face of societal structures that limit their possibilities
and well-being. Entering into the Word of scripture has transformed
their understanding of what it means to be a follower of Christ. On
the other hand, a community of upper-middle-class North Americans may realize by reading the same scripture that they have become
entangled in the prosperity gospel, justifying material accumulation
under the auspices of God's will — an interpretation that is difficult
to support by means of the overarching message of scripture.

As individuals, the spiritual-theological dimension can have a profound impact upon the way we live our lives and the choices we make.
For someone experiencing a time of spiritual dryness, a "dark night
of the soul" as described by Saint John of the Cross, the whole book
of Isaiah might speak about this feeling of separation from the living
God, all the while extending the personal hope of restoration to God's
presence. Perhaps reading the narratives about Jesus of Nazareth, his
life and ministry, may lead someone to abandon their career as a corporate executive and devote themselves to a nonprofit organization
that seeks to promote preservation of the environment or to develop
educational opportunities generating hope for the future in inner-city
children.

As these examples illustrate, learning to read, interpret, and live out the spiritual-theological level requires that we remain open to hearing a word in the text that we have not heard before, being willing to "test out" the truth-bearing possibility of our interpretation. This openness means that we cannot expect to find or hold onto "the" meaning and truth of the text — an expectation that is not uncommon when reading at the historical-descriptive and moral-prescriptive levels of interpretation only. Instead, when we enter the Scriptures at all three levels, we realize that the word we receive is provisional, in a sense, because grace meets us where we are and leads us where we hope to go in our faith journey: toward the destination of love. We read the Scriptures as a community of Christ's followers because we want to draw nearer to God and to become better followers of Christ in all circumstances of our lives. If we seek to discern God's will, then we must be willing to let go of our preconceived notions from time to time. Thus, the spiritual-theological level requires us to be in the process of growth and transformation, rather than clinging to a final judgment on what a particular text is saying. We are not "saved" by knowing the Scriptures, but we are in the process of being remade in the likeness of the living God and having the Christ-character formed in us. Christian life in God is a process, not a product; it is a journey, not a destination.

The above descriptions of the importance of the Bible to the life of faith and of the contemporary skepticism and perpetuation of myth are intended to bring to light a central assumption: Today, as in earlier generations, we are consumed by the question of what constitutes a good life and how we might live such a life. As old as recorded history, this question continues to pervade our sensibilities in the twenty-first century. We seek to live a good life, and as Christians, we understand the good life to be related to our participation in God. Such participation, however, requires that we receive and embody God's grace, especially in the form of these three: faith, hope, and love. We need, then, to deepen our understanding of the theological virtues.

THE RISE OF THE THEOLOGICAL VIRTUES

Asking about the relationship of the theological virtues to one another and their importance in the Christian life does not begin in a vacuum. A significant history of the virtues can be traced from the classical ideas of Greek philosophy through the early Christian writers into the Middle Ages and the Reformation. In the following pages, we focus on four central figures in the rise and development of the Christian understanding of faith, hope, and love: Plato, Aristotle, Augustine, and Aquinas. While others have dealt with the notion of virtue and the theological virtues, a look at these four enables us to grasp the problems and possibilities associated with a renewal of the meaning and significance of faith, hope, and love.

To examine the emergence of the theological virtues and their importance to the Christian journey requires us to return to a time and world before the birth of Jesus of Nazareth, as the roots of the virtues are found in ancient Greece.[7] In particular, the philosophies of Plato (ca. 428–347 B.C.E.) and Aristotle (384–322 B.C.E.) set the framework for our discussion, as they represent the most influential of the Greek philosophers in the development of virtue theory. While both are concerned with the source and conduct of the good life in its holistic expression, their approaches to the nature and role of the virtues in attaining the good life unfold in distinctive manners.

The Virtues of Plato

To examine Plato's approach to the virtues and the good life, we need to begin, briefly, with his teacher, Socrates, for whom the pursuit of the good life is the end or goal of human existence. The good life that we seek, the fullest expression of our human existence, is known as *eudaimonia,* a word that is translated imprecisely into English as happiness, blessedness, or contentment. For the Greeks, however, *eudaimonia* meant more than the sort of happiness commonly sought in contemporary society. It is not about the acquisition of wealth, fame, or power as ends in themselves. It is not about simply feeling "good."

Rather, for the Greeks, *eudaimonia* expresses human flourishing; it suggests that a human being is fulfilling his or her potential; it means becoming as fully human as we can be. Such fulfillment of each person's potential is a function of the life of virtue or *arête,* which might best be thought of as the superior qualities or excellences of a good life, rather than simply as moral rectitude. Among the virtues, wisdom or practical knowledge, *phronesis,* was deemed by Socrates to be the most important because it enables a person to choose what is right, and once we know what is morally right, we do it. Thus, the key to the good life, to human flourishing, is the individual cultivation of virtue, and especially wisdom, through education.

Although Plato drew upon and was shaped by his teacher's work, he departed from Socrates' emphasis upon knowledge as the primary virtue in our pursuit of the good life. Instead, in his most significant dialogue, the *Republic,* Plato presents justice as the fundamental virtue of both the state and individuals, though the virtues of wisdom, courage, and moderation are also vitally important. On the communal level, Plato asserts that for the just state to exist, each person must perform the work or function to which he or she is best suited by nature. Plato's schema separates persons into three classes which, when properly ordered, compose a harmonious whole: the rulers or "guardians" who possess wisdom; the warriors or "auxiliaries" who possess courage, and the most common of the classes, the workers or laborers, who are most closely associated with the virtue of moderation. When each person fulfills the function that is truest to his or her own nature, then justice, the highest of the virtues, may be realized for the state as a whole. To be sure, in our contemporary setting, we would critique the hierarchical nature of Plato's schema and draw attention to his lack of concern for upward mobility and equal opportunity as we understand them today. Yet his goal of justice is one that we still consider to be essential to the good life.

In similar fashion to this conception of the ideal city-state, the just individual consists of a tripartite soul: the "rational part," reason and wisdom, which approximates the ruling class; the affective or "spirited part," which is the seat of courage and relates to the guardians; and the appetitive part, which is the location of temperance or moderation and corresponds to the class of laborers. By cultivating the virtues of the well-ordered soul, in which the mind and reason rule or dominate the emotions and appetites, a person can flourish and live a good life. Thus, for Plato, the key to both the good life and the good society begins with the individual who seeks to fulfill his or her nature most fully; cultivates the virtues of wisdom, courage, moderation, and justice; and lives a rightly ordered life.

The Virtues of Aristotle

In *The Nichomachean Ethics,* Aristotle, like Plato, is concerned with human flourishing, *eudaimonia,* as the goal of human life and the reason for cultivating the virtues. He examines three possible forms of the good life, suggesting it may consist of pleasure, politics, or contemplation. The goal of the life of pleasure is to satisfy the basic human appetites. This form of the "good life" does not require the exercise of reason and thus, argues Aristotle, is little better than the life lived by lower animals. The goal of the political life is honor, yet honor is conferred by others rather than internal to the individual, which means people "seem to pursue honor in order that they may be assured of their [own] merit;..."[8] In other words, those who seek honor are motivated by external rewards that somehow prove their worth or value as persons, rather than seeking the happiness that is intrinsic to their nature. For Aristotle, only the life of contemplation has a goal that is "self-sufficient" and thereby able to produce human flourishing. Only the way of contemplation can lead to the good life.

Contemplation, which is defined as an intellectual activity, has four features that render it the most valuable of all human activities: appropriateness, pleasantness, continuity, and self-sufficiency. According to Aristotle, "that which is proper to each thing is by nature best and most pleasant for each thing; for man, therefore, the life according to intellect is best and pleasantest, since intellect more than anything else *is* man."[9] In addition to being proper and pleasant to the human being, this intellectual activity is "the most continuous, since we can contemplate truth more continuously than we can *do* anything."[10] Finally, contemplation has the distinction of being the most self-sufficient activity, as it is loved for its own sake and has no end beyond itself.

In light of the significance Aristotle places on intellectual activity, he conceptualizes the soul as consisting of two parts: the rational, which is the highest form of human activity, and the irrational, which is further divided into a "vegetative" part that causes nourishment and growth and an "appetitive" part that can be persuaded by the rational part of the soul. In keeping with this dichotomy, there are intellectual virtues, such as understanding and practical wisdom, and moral virtues, which belong to the irrational part of the soul. Of particular importance among these various virtues is practical wisdom, *phronesis,* because its goal is action, not simply understanding. For Aristotle, the best course of action, when guided by practical wisdom, involves neither excess nor deficiency, but aims at the mean.[11] The moral virtues such as the "mean" dispositions of courage, temperance, friendliness, justice, modesty, and generosity are integral to the good life; however, they result from the deliberation and choice of the rational part of the soul. Thus, the exercise of practical wisdom or right action, in and through the activity of contemplation or right understanding, is the source of human flourishing or the good life. Practical wisdom is essential to living the good life, because we are most fully human when we exercise our intellectual virtues to guide our conduct.

The good life is also dependent, to some extent, upon the practical wisdom of the particular individual in concrete circumstances, for virtuous choice seeks the mean that "is neither too much nor too little — and this is not one, nor the same for all."[12] In a manner similar to Plato's view, Aristotle recognizes that different persons have different qualities or degrees of qualities, and the development of these virtues must be consistent with their own nature. For example, what constitutes the mean of "courage" or that of "temperance" differs depending upon the person and the context in which the person must choose the mean. To be more specific, in the case of the consumption of food, the mean of the virtue of moderation differs considerably depending upon whether one is a jockey or a middle linebacker in the NFL. Aristotle, like Plato before him, also considered the good life as being within the grasp of each individual through careful formation. By means of instruction and repetition, a person's character can be shaped to be virtuous, and once the character is formed, it is an ongoing source of good actions because the person both knows what is right and does it. In other words, by nature the human being — or at least the human being born into the right social class who has the time and leisure to pursue the philosophical life and the means to receive the proper education — has the capacity to achieve the good life.

The Christian Virtues of Augustine

Where the Greek philosophers fall short in their understanding of the good life, according to the Christian perspective, is expressed well by Augustine, the bishop of Hippo (354–430 C.E.). His account of the virtues and the good life is most developed in his "handbook," *Enchiridion on Faith, Hope, and Love* and his monumental work, *The City of God*. Augustine, of course, lived in a time when the influence of Greek and Roman philosophies was pronounced; his own "Christian philosophy," or what we would call "theology," takes certain aspects of the Greek understanding into account, especially because philosophy and contemplation, the life of the mind, continued to be highly esteemed. In his pursuit of what constitutes the good life, Augustine, like the Greeks, believed that the soul of the human being had to be rightly ordered, and the reasoned mind played an important role in this ordering. Again, proper training and practice are necessary conditions. A person must be instructed in the doctrines or teachings of the faith in order to avoid error and to appropriate and live the Christian life. According to Augustine, then, a proper understanding of faith, hope, and love leads to the question, "to what extent religion is supported by reason... "[13] Here, in a departure from Plato and Aristotle, Augustine places limits upon the role of reason in cultivating the good life and brings to light the grace of God as present in faith, hope, and love. Reason, in and of itself, cannot lead us to happiness or the good life because such a life is found where faith, hope, and love flourish.

Although a full treatment of his argument is not possible in this brief overview, three significant points highlight his concern to depart from the Greek philosophical tradition: (1) the nature of the will, (2) the humble way of Christ, and (3) the wisdom of scripture. One of Augustine's central teachings concerns the free will of human beings, especially under the condition of original sin. The human will is the source of good and evil in human beings and, imprisoned in the grip of fallen nature, the will cannot do the good it wishes to do. Our choices are, in fact, constrained by our nature: "Our wills are ours and it is our wills that affect all that we do by willing.... And yet a [person's] life cannot be right without a right belief in God."[14] In other words, reason may tell us the best course of action, but our wills are not free not to sin. New Year's resolutions are a good example of how the best intentions often fall short. Thus, the good life cannot be achieved by human means alone. Contemplation and the formation of practical wisdom to guide proper conduct are insufficient to bring about human flourishing and happiness. Belief in God is a prerequisite.

Second, in an interesting argument from *The City of God,* Augustine praises the Neoplatonic ("Platonist") philosophers such as Plotinus (205–70 c.e.) and Porphyry (232–305 c.e.) who are near-Christians, yet lack the one thing necessary: faith in Christ. Augustine writes of Porphyry that he professes "to be a lover of virtue and wisdom," but if he were actually a lover of these things, then he "would have recognized 'Christ, the Power of God and the Wisdom of God', instead of shying away from his saving humility, inflated with the swollen pride of useless learning."[15] The Platonists, in Augustine's view, were blinded by pride as they tried to lift themselves up by their own intellectual efforts. They could not see that true wisdom, the true source of living the good life, is found in Christ who is the Word become flesh. Augustine concludes that the Greek philosophical tradition exalts human wisdom and strength, but the humility of Christ's incarnation shows us a way that diverges directly from that intellectual tradition. Augustine thus argues that we cannot find the way to God and the good life of happiness by means of our own efforts. Yet, by grace, God has been revealed to us in the form of Jesus Christ, giving us the way that leads us toward the goal of happiness and the good life. In other words, for all that the philosophers claimed rightly and well, they lacked the one thing needed: the humble way of Christ, the living God. This is the way of faith in which we acknowledge that we need help to arrive at the desired destination. It is also important to note that, for Augustine, the way of Christ is available to all, not just those who possess the greatest powers of reasoning or the luxury of the philosophical life.

A third divergence from the Greek philosophical tradition concerns the authority of the Scriptures, an understanding that we inherit from the Hebrew tradition. Although the fixed canon of Christian biblical texts was still in the process of being determined in Augustine's time, the gist of his argument remains relevant, despite our contemporary uneasiness with the concept of "authority." The Scriptures, claims Augustine, "are the writings of outstanding authority in which we put our trust concerning those things which we need to know for our good, and yet are incapable of discovering by ourselves."[16] In other words, the revelatory power of the Scriptures is unique; the Bible bears witness to the wisdom and way of Christ, and we cannot find our way to happiness without it. Our reason alone cannot discover the truths that are revealed by the Word of God in scripture. As he emphasizes in *On Christian Doctrine,* those who seek the will of God turn to the instruction of the Holy Scriptures, and although the writings are not without ambiguities and uncertainties, we can be taught to read and interpret them. One need only glance at Augustine's writings or his many extant sermons to recognize the authoritative — though not literal — word that he understands the Scriptures contain. The Scriptures serve to guide our restless hearts toward the destination of home; without them, we lack access to the witness and wisdom of Christ and his way.

Augustine, then, redirects our understanding of the virtues and their role in cultivating the good life. The life of moral virtue is beyond our grasp because of the power of sin imprisoning or undermining our free will. Of our own efforts and knowledge, we cannot attain the good life. We must humbly accept the gift of restoration that is offered in and by Christ. The Triune God is the sole source of the good life and "participation in him brings happiness to all who are happy in truth.... "[17] Moreover, Augustine argues that the virtues, or excellences of human life, "can exist only in those in whom true godliness is present," but they do not prevent misfortunes from befalling the bearer of such genuine virtues.[18] To suggest that we can be free from suffering by cultivating the virtues is, for Augustine, sheer folly. To suppose that we can attain happiness by means of intellectual contemplation or moral virtue denies the reality of our human nature and our need for God's gracious assistance. The good life is lived on the basis of faith, hope, and love by which we receive the "power to live rightly," and it can only be found in Christ through the scriptural witnesses.[19]

The Christian Virtues of Aquinas

This transition from the Greek philosophical virtue tradition to the Christian perspective of Augustine leads us, finally, to consider the refinements and clarifications offered by Thomas Aquinas in the thirteenth century. Both Aristotle and Augustine were influences on the philosophical theology of Aquinas. Like Augustine, he upholds the authority of scripture, as it provides us with God's revelation made to the apostles and prophets, and he believes that reason alone cannot provide complete knowledge of the divine. Aquinas also accepts that the human will in the state of nature is corrupted by original sin. Like Aristotle, he is concerned that people and things should fulfill their proper function or true nature, and he maintains that virtues are habits or dispositions that serve to make us better and lead us toward the good life. Yet Aquinas's conception of the virtues and their role in helping us achieve the good life adds considerably to the development of the unique role of faith, hope, and love in the Christian life. Here, he distinguishes the intellectual and moral virtues from the theological virtues and differentiates the natural from the supernatural virtues. This refinement or deepening of the theological virtues helps facilitate the renewal of faith, hope, and love in the contemporary context.

For Aquinas a virtue is a habit that disposes us to perform good actions, in conformity with reason, and enables us to realize our full human potential. We are able to act in accordance with the good when we exhibit both intellectual virtues (i.e., well-disposed reason) and moral virtues (i.e., neither excess nor deficiency in our appetites). This combination of the intellectual and moral virtues, then, most perfectly fulfills the definition of virtue or human excellence as, together, they enable us both to know and to do what is right. The "cardinal virtues" of justice, temperance, courage, and prudence — three moral and one intellectual — play a pivotal role in leading us toward the good life. Thus, Aquinas agrees with those who preceded him that human flourishing is a matter of ordering our actions toward proper ends. Morality, or right conduct, is a personal act, but Aquinas is clear that our actions do have social consequences — something that Aristotle did not fully accept. Here Aquinas argues that right conduct means, at times, we must choose to limit ourselves for the good of others. Aquinas, like Augustine before him, also departed from Aristotelian virtue ethics by including the Christian disposition of humility among the virtues.

Aquinas's understanding of the cardinal virtues also brings to light the role played by the gifts of free will and reason. Because the human will is defective, our intention to act rightly cannot ensure that, in fact, our actions will be good. Though we can develop and cultivate the natural virtues through learning and practice, they are insufficient to lead us to the good life. Only by and through the grace of God are we able to exercise the cardinal virtue of prudence in the service of justice, temperance, and courage, and thereby do what leads to human flourishing. In other words, when we act as fully rational and free creatures in pursuit of the good life, we most closely reflect the image of God within us. As Etienne Gilson has expressed it, God is both free and rational, and these activities set the human creature apart from other living things. Thus, we are most fully human when we are in the image of God.[20] The cardinal virtues alone, however, do not bring about human flourishing or excellence. For Aquinas, the theological virtues must also be present in us.

Because the human will remains subject to the power of sin, the cardinal virtues require the infusion of the grace of God in the form of the theological virtues of faith, hope, and love. The object of these three virtues is always and only God, and this end or goal is what sets them apart as theological virtues. They are not given by nature, but are infused by grace, which, in Aquinas's words, "is the greatest good simply speaking, since by it a man is ordered to the highest good, which is God."[21] In other words, without God's grace, we have a palette of paints, but no brush by which to fill the canvas of our lives. Thus, whereas the moral virtues are a mixture of the natural and supernatural elements, the theological virtues are strictly gifts of the Spirit that point toward God as their sole end and enable us to prioritize our lives accordingly. Gilson explains it in this way: "The supernatural moral virtues allow [a person] to act *for God;* the theological virtues allow him to act *with God* and *in God.*"[22] We might say that faith, hope, and love enable us to participate in God in Christ in the Holy Spirit. Without these three gifts, we can only develop the measure of goodness that resides in us by nature, but that goodness will not be able to bring about the good life we seek. The theological virtues thus dispose a person toward the ultimate Good and the fullness of human flourishing, as Aquinas claims in his *Disputed Questions on the Virtues in General:*

In order that we be moved correctly to the end, the end must be known and desired. But the desire of the end requires two things, namely, trust concerning the end to be obtained, because no wise man moves toward that which he cannot attain, and love of the end, because only the loved is desired. There are accordingly three theological virtues, namely, faith, by which we know God, hope, whereby we hope to attain him, and charity, by which we love him.[23]

In sum, Aquinas develops our understanding of the theological virtues as he argues that, by nature, we can do a certain amount of good and can be good people, to an extent, but we cannot develop the fullest potential of our humanity or live the good life without the grace of God given to us in the form of faith, hope, and love. These three are the virtues that can lead us through the suffering and pain of this world toward the happiness we seek, as they enable us to participate in God in Christ in the Holy Spirit.

RECOVERING A THEOLOGICAL UNDERSTANDING OF HUMAN FLOURISHING

This brief summary of the rise and development of the theological virtues in the Christian tradition enables us to glean the wisdom of the past in order to move constructively toward locating faith, hope, and love within our contemporary context. The writings of Plato, Aristotle, Augustine, and Aquinas help us to discern four basic ways in which the theological virtues serve to guide our search for the good life and human flourishing. In particular, the tradition points us toward (1) the problematic language of "virtue"; (2) the inherent relationality of faith, hope, and love; (3) their role in Christian formation; and (4) the importance of the scriptural witnesses for the Christian journey toward God.

The first insight gleaned from the tradition is that the language of "virtue" has become quite problematic. In contemporary usage, the concept is most readily identified with concerns about the moral behavior of human beings and has become separated from the earlier meaning of virtue as human excellence and flourishing. If we accept that, by nature, we are unable to achieve the good we seek, then the goal of moral virtue is ambiguous and elusive, at best, and prone to cultivate pharisaical self-righteousness, at worst. We need to recover the understanding of virtue as that which epitomizes and composes what makes us most fully human and that, in fact, we are most fully human in the image of God. The grace of God given in the form of the theological virtues of faith, hope, and love are, therefore, essential to our full humanity and to living the good life as good people. As we proceed through the subsequent chapters, rather than attempting to redefine "virtue" in its earlier sense, we speak of faith, hope, and love as those qualities of excellence received by grace and manifested in the Christ-character within us.

When we speak of these three excellences, we are directed toward a second insight: Faith, hope, and love are inherently relational qualities. By nature, they exist as a threesome and cannot be separated, if we hope to flourish as human beings. This inherent relationality says a great deal about the Christian life. The three grace-filled excellences enable us to participate in God and the good life, and as such, they constitute our lifelines to God, as if an umbilical cord connecting us to the divine life. Yet faith, hope, and love not only connect us to God, but they form a fabric or web that weaves us together with one another and the whole of creation, in and through the grace of God in Christ in the Holy Spirit. Relationship and community are basic to the nature of God, and the good life participates in these qualities, thus suggesting that the good life is lived in community and for the benefit of all. Faith, hope, and love thus empower and enliven our Christ-character and enable us to live as wise, just, generous, kind, courageous, moderate people — or at least to gradually develop such characteristics over a lifetime of trusting in God and participating in the Christian life. Indeed, faith, hope, and love, themselves, are relational, as they function together to guide and deepen the journey of faith. We are called to live according to the influence and guidance of all three of these qualities working in concert. Life in God in Christ in the Holy Spirit is unmistakably and irreducibly relational, and faith, hope, and love are the ties that hold the delicate web together, stretched at times, but not broken.

In recognizing the inherently relational nature of faith, hope, and love and the web into which we are drawn, a third insight is recovered: formation of the Christ-character over time, through education and practice. As the Greeks and Augustine so clearly emphasized, the development of our full potential as human beings requires formation. We might suggest that, today, this formation involves both an education into the basic beliefs of the Christian faith, a training of the intellect, and the cultivation of habits or practices that enable us to embody and live out those teachings. The mind, body, and spirit of the person are formed within the Christian community and in the presence of grace in the form of faith, hope, and love. Without these three gifts, the formation of our human potential into the likeness of God falls short of the mark. Yet there exists a symbiotic relationship between our human efforts at formation and the guidance and revelatory power of grace, for we must both cultivate a deep intellectual understanding of the Christian life and rely upon the means of grace such as prayer, worship, outreach, and the study of scripture to allow faith, hope, and love to work in and through us and to shape each of us into the people God created us to be.

As we realize the importance of formation and Christian practices, we come once again to the centrality of the Scriptures in the life of faith. In the Bible, and especially the witnesses of the New Testament, we find the signposts of faith, hope, and love to guide us toward our destination of the good life, the fully human life in the image of God. If we do not participate in the wisdom and witness of scripture at all three levels of interpretation, and on a regular basis, then we have little possibility of participating in the reality of God in Christ in the Holy Spirit at the deepest and most fully human dimension. In the witnesses of the Scriptures, we find that the Christ-character, the fullness of human flourishing, is inextricably related to our love of God and others and to our compassion and actions toward those who are least valued by our society. We find that the gifts of faith, hope, and love are given to us so that as we become fully human, we participate in the flourishing of the whole of creation.

As we turn now to each of the three qualities of excellence, the guidance of the early tradition of the theological virtues enables us, first, to examine the ways in which our contemporary context distorts and misuses faith, hope, and love, and, second, to consider where they are yet located within the North American context.

Chapter Three

FAITH IN GOD

As Christians, faith in God is essential to living the good life. From Abraham's travels and travails to the encouragement of Revelation to "hold on!" in the midst of persecution, the Scriptures bear witness to the centrality of faith. From the earliest Christians gathered in house churches to the newest communities springing up in Asia and Africa, followers of Christ, in continuity with the scriptural witnesses, have proclaimed the importance of having vital, living faith in God in Christ in the Holy Spirit. Yet today, even as pronouncements about "faith" seem to flow freely, the meaning of faith in God has become increasingly diluted and misdirected toward alternative expressions to those found in the Scriptures and the witness of later generations of Christians.

Four significant trends complicate our ability to understand the reality of Christian faith in the contemporary era and beckon numerous would-be disciples down paths leading away from the reality of God. Such misdirection of the journey is always subtle; it makes us think we are following God's way or pursuing the good life, when we are actually doing otherwise. The language of faith may be used, but the source and goal of faith, God, is misplaced. The first trend relates to the rise of science and technology as avenues to positing truth claims and promoting progress toward the good; the second places faith in persons; the third highlights the privatization of faith in the form of "Jesus is my personal Lord and Savior"; and the fourth seeks benefits without any commitment or response required. The first two trends relate to the desire to be guided by some external authority, what Paul Tillich called, "heteronomy"; the latter are expressions of the desire for "autonomy," the ultimacy of internal authority. Examining these missteps enables us to consider what it means to be guided by faith in God, Tillich's "theonomy," and how such faith may be located and conceptualized in contemporary North America.

FOUR CONTEMPORARY DISTORTIONS OF FAITH

The Scientific Option

Over the past century, science and technology have transformed our ordinary lives in extraordinary ways. We need not probe too deeply to find evidence of this fact; advancements in transportation, for example, have been nothing short of stunning. In December 1903, Wilbur and Orville Wright flew a mere 120 feet off a hillside in Kitty Hawk, North Carolina; five years later, Henry Ford rolled out his first model T. By mid-century, transportation technologies were skyrocketing: the 1960s were driven by the race to conquer space and culminated in the moment when Neil Armstrong set foot on the surface of the moon. Today, space tourists are paying stupendous sums of money for the opportunity to stare out the window of the international space station. The point is clear: the shape of life in North America has experienced and continues to undergo a radical transformation, which extends into virtually every area of our lives. As Ray Kurzweil notes, "The last century has seen enormous technological change and the social upheavals that go along with it, which few pundits circa 1899 foresaw. The pace of change is accelerating.... The result will be far greater transformation in the first two decades of the twenty-first century than we saw in the entire twentieth century."[1] From an uncritical perspective, the possibility for improvements in the quantity and quality of life seems greater than ever — virtually unlimited.

In any room of a modern American home, on any corner of any street, even high atop a mountain where climbers decked in Gore-Tex scan the heavens as a Boeing 767 roars past, the changes wrought by science and technology permeate our society and day-to-day lives. From microwave popcorn to miracle drugs, all-wheel-drive behemoths to the World Wide Web, CNN twenty-four-hour news to disposable diapers, the fruits of our scientific and technological advances are woven, almost seamlessly, into the fabric of our existence. With such wonders, even miracles, enveloping our every moment, faith in God increasingly appears as a poor and unnecessary means of pursuing the good life, a relic passed down by our more primitive Christian ancestors. Why put our faith in an unseen God, when today we can touch, taste, feel, hear, and see, as well as benefit from, the endless creativity of the human mind?

Thus, the first contemporary "faith" trend is the scientific option in which we place our trust and expectation for discovering the good life in human knowledge and the human creative potential. But Christian faith, according to the scriptural and historical understanding, is placed in that which is unseen: "Now faith is the assurance of things hoped for, the conviction of things not seen" (Heb. 11:1). When we place our faith in the works of human hands, in those things that we can see and touch, we deceive ourselves, for the "evidence" of progress toward the good life by means of human creativity is an illusion. At the core of our lives, things are not remarkably better than they were a hundred years ago; they are simply different.

Rather than proving to be the solution to what ails us, science and technology are not unequivocally good, but a mixture of good and bad. While we marvel at the advances and improvements in our lives, we cannot help but notice the other side of the story. The Internet, for example, has increased the speed and lowered the cost of written communications, and it has widened the availability of research data and information. Yet, at the same time, we cannot deny the unintended consequences of our computerization: the constant barrage of unwanted messages and advertisements, the decrease in human contact, the limited access available to the poor, the increased likelihood that our communication will be misunderstood, and the easy access that minors now have to violent and pornographic materials. The list of scientific and technological advances that warrant a less-than-ideal appraisal is endless: the mass production of food, including fast food of limited nutritional value that is linked to the rise in obesity and a host of health problems; the proliferation of nuclear, biological, and chemical weapons; airliners used as weapons of mass destruction; television simultaneously providing mindless entertainment and real-time transmissions of tragedies, such that we become desensitized to suffering and death; the modern automobile that idles for hours on overcrowded freeways spewing toxic wastes into the air. Undoubtedly, faith in science and technology as the means to create the good life is an illusion or, at best, a good that is inevitably misused or uncontrollable in the hands of human beings.

There is little doubt that science and technology are an important part of our contemporary life, and the role they play will continue to shape and impact society. Nevertheless, because we cannot factor out the human element, these things cannot bring us to the good life for which we yearn. They cannot create more time for our overcrowded lives; they cannot hold suffering and death at bay, ultimately. The fruits of our creative labors contribute to a growing sense of loneliness and alienation, to the loss of community and social capital that are now reaching epidemic proportions in the United States. Like human life itself, our creativity is a mixture of good and bad. It, too, is subject to the brokenness of our existence.

Christian faith is not and cannot be faith in human achievements or in the potential of the creative human spirit to discover the answers to the human condition. Rather, Christian faith is located always and only in the living God in Christ in the Holy Spirit, in whom the human condition is overcome, though it awaits historical completion. There is no middle ground; our faith as Christians is faith in the living God or it is misplaced, idolatrous faith. Paul Tillich long ago argued that the holy can be either divine or demonic, depending on whether or not our faith is idolatrous, that is, faith in which the finite claims infinity.[2] Using Tillich's way of framing the argument, faith in ourselves, in science, in technology, in amassing wealth, and so forth, is idolatrous faith because it is faith in that which is less than the reality of God. Although for many persons, placing faith in such things has to do with the fact that science and technology are based upon hard data and replicable results, in reality, any demand for some form of concrete evidence becomes a temptation to turn away from God, not a surer foundation upon which to build our future. People of faith would do well to remember that scientists are often the first to acknowledge there is a good deal of guesswork involved in their ability to "prove" many assumptions we hold to be true. Given further study, the understanding may undergo radical revision. Such is the case in theoretical physics where, in isolation from one another, the theories of special relativity and quantum mechanics both possess explanatory power; however, they are incommensurable discourses that do not mesh into one overarching theory. Both cannot be true, at least in terms of our current knowledge.

In this first "faith" trend, then, epistemological concerns are central, and reason becomes the primary source for faith. Intelligent persons seek to find a surer foundation for pursuing the good than can be provided by the unseen. Skeptics and scientists, educated and literate, these persons find it difficult to accept the mythological worldview of scripture as offering a glimpse of reality and tend to view it as a prescientific explanatory model. The scriptural narrative seems irreconcilable with contemporary knowledge. Here "faith" seeks a better explanatory model than the etiological tales and moral prescriptions of scripture can provide — one that stands up to rigorous scientific and academic standards, one that provides some rational, provable basis for living our lives. Persons subscribing to this "faith" trend may feel more comfortable participating in communities where sermons are less biblically oriented and, instead, focus on examples of the "good life" drawn from literature, science, and human history. Of course, the Scriptures are not so much an "explanatory model" of our human life together as they are a source of God's grace, empowerment, and direction for living in the world with a stake in the future reconciliation of all things. Seeking to locate epistemological claims in an external authority based upon replicable truth claims, the scientific option places faith in the human being and its creative potential. Although there is much to be said for human creativity working in concert with divine creativity, in denying or rejecting the reality of the living God, whether from a deistic or agnostic perspective, the good we seek and the flourishing of human life remain elusive.

The Expert-Witness Option

The second distortion of faith in the contemporary era represents an alternative means of locating faith in an external authority. This trend represents a hierarchical and more traditional model of faith, in which persons place their faith in the institution to which they belong or, even more narrowly, in a particular pastor or any individual person — something or someone to whom they can look up and feel secure in their beliefs. Here faith is placed in the reliability and credibility of an "expert witness." This distortion can manifest itself in a variety of forms, anything from an unquestioning obedience to the teachings of a particular denomination to following an itinerating pastor from church to church to placing faith in the wisdom and dependability of our spouse to know the truth that will lead us toward the good life. In this expression of faith, we want someone or some community to provide us with a sure foundation upon which to build our future — that "old time religion" is good enough for me.

In this second distortion, the epistemological concerns are primary, yet quite distinct from those of the scientific option. People who follow this form of faith are seeking someone or something "closer" to God than they are; they want someone to provide the truth, to offer the simple answers that will lead them to the good life. Here tradition, rather than reason, often becomes the overarching norm for faith, though at times under the auspices of the authority of scripture. Ambiguity and doubt have no place in the Christian life, and either-or maxims reign. For example, we either have faith or do not, such that there can be no degrees of faith, no deepening of faith, and no questioning of the official teachings allowed. In this case, all that happens, whether for good or ill, is simply ascribed to "God's will." Thus, in the hierarchical faith option, the hermeneutic dimension of life together and the reality of interpreting scripture are seldom acknowledged. The Word of God is often viewed as an unvarying and absolute authority because we have a written document handed down from one generation to the next. The church and its leadership, informed by the Holy Spirit, simply share what they have read in a relatively straightforward manner. What the church proclaims is thus equated with God's own law and Word, which must be followed in order to secure the good life.

This form of faith, however, neglects to take seriously the distinction that always exists between the creature and the Creator, and the inevitable reality that no human being or institution is infallible, no matter how sincere the intentions of that leadership may be. No human being or institution can resolve the paradoxical, ambiguous reality of God with and beyond us; we can only strive to bring to light what God reveals to us in history. Even so, our knowledge of the things of God is limited by our finitude. When seminary students or church members are asked if they believe the pope is fallible, they are always quick to point out that all popes past, present, and future are human and make mistakes. Yet, at times, these same persons fiercely defend their own churches or pastors as offering the "true path" that leads to life, as if the authority they place themselves under cannot but possess the unmitigated truth. The reality of human brokenness means, however, that no person or institution can lead us to the good life or can serve as an unfailing source of truth in our lives. Sooner or later, any external authority will fall short of leading us to the good that we seek, no matter how well-intentioned or wise it may be. Even the Scriptures, when held up as the indisputable, inerrant, perfect Word of God, become an idol of our own making and lead us away from the reality we so desperately seek to embrace and embody. Placing our faith in an "expert witness" provides a false sense of security in our knowledge of the "truth," as it subtly leads us away from God in Jesus Christ in the Holy Spirit.

The Jesus-in-My-Heart Option

The third distortion of faith, the Jesus-in-my-heart option, points in a very different direction, that of privatizing faith, though the results are similar. Central to this distortion is the claim that "Jesus is my personal Lord and Savior" — what Robert Bellah suggests comes dangerously close to asserting "the individual as the preeminent being in the universe."[3] The Jesus-in-my-heart form of faith places an emphasis upon personal experience as a sure foundation to the Christian way. Epistemologically, empiricism is central in this option. "Faith" involves little more than the personal confession of Jesus Christ that results in the individual's salvation, goodness, eternal life. The logic of the "Jesus is my personal Lord and Savior" faith runs something like this: I express my faith in Jesus, Jesus then dwells in my heart, and I am forgiven and saved once and for all time. The stress here falls on the individual as the subject, thereby denying that, in faith, we are called to open ourselves to God's will and way and to agree to become the object of God's grace and to make God the object of our faith, thereby ceasing to place ourselves first. This option denies that, in faith, we remain human and broken, though graced by our relationship with God. While this faith option revels in "possessing" Jesus within, it neglects the reality of faith by which we are "possessed" by the living God. Ours is not to be given Jesus in our hearts, but to open our hearts and to share Christ with others. In this Jesus-in-my-heart option, faith is about living the good life now and feeling good. It is a faith that expects God to fulfill our personal desires immediately, such that the good life is at hand.

A prime example of this version of the privatization of faith is found in the best-selling book *The Prayer of Jabez,* in which God becomes an on-demand deity, requiring only that we know the secret word to win the prize, in a manner of speaking.[4] According to Wilkinson's interpretation of the one obscure reference to Jabez in 1 Chronicles 4:11, if we learn to pray in the right way, God will bless us with great wealth and societal success. This book, however, neglects to consider that when the disciples asked Jesus to teach them how to pray, he did not point them to Jabez's prayer, but taught to them what we know as the Lord's Prayer. In fact, we need not dig too deeply before we discover that the author's interpretation is antithetical to the Lord's Prayer. Jesus of Nazareth teaches us to pray for "our daily bread," not for a lifetime supply. He teaches his disciples to pray for God's will to be done, not their own will. Moreover, *The Prayer of Jabez* fails to count the cost to others when our personal, individual prayers are "answered."[5]

In a rather glaring example, Wilkinson recounts the story of praying for his airline flight to be delayed on an occasion when he was running late.[6] When the flight is miraculously postponed, he finds himself sitting at the gate in conversation with a woman going through a divorce. He concludes that his prayer not only allowed him to make his flight, but also to be in ministry to her, yet Wilkinson fails to give a moment's thought to the dozens of other people on that flight and how their lives might have been impacted by his personal desire to make the flight through its late departure. Perhaps someone was rushing to the deathbed of a parent, and the delay kept them from saying a final "I love you." Perhaps someone missed his child's first recital, which he had promised to attend. Perhaps the delay cost the airline thousands of dollars that would eventually be absorbed by passengers paying higher prices for their tickets. Would these things have been God's will so that Wilkinson could make his flight? It is unfortunate that the *Prayer of Jabez* has evidently generated a substantial amount of misplaced faith in persons who are genuine in their desire to nurture their faith. But when "faith" becomes a form of individualism and personal prosperity under the guise of Christian discipleship, the good life and human flourishing are diminished.

   The privatization of faith is certainly not a new phenomenon even
as the Jesus-in-my-heart version represents a new twist on the old
theme. Liberal theology is noted for having relegated religion to the
private realm, though such segmentation is antithetical to contemporary theologies that illuminate the centrality of praxis and the public
role of religion. In the biblical witnesses, faith turns us away from a
self-centered existence, enabling us to be present for others as a vital
part of the larger community and greater good, though a complete
sacrifice of the self is not implied, a point to which we return subsequently. Moreover, in liberal theology and the nineteenth-century
German philosophy upon which it was built, the immanence of God
was primary, epitomized by Hegel's concept of the "immanent spirit"
or God manifest in the German *Volk*. The contemporary U.S. version
goes one step further by locating the Spirit of God within the individual believer, rather than in the people or the nation as a whole, even
as U.S. leaders continue to use the rhetoric of God manifest in the
American people. Here again, Delbanco's thesis, suggesting that the
guiding American vision has shifted from the nation to the individual as the repository of God's Spirit and will, comes into view. Faith
has become "my" faith in God; the community is a corollary to the
primacy of what already exists within me. Thus, the brokenness of
life remains undiminished, though the language of wholeness is used.

   In this distortion of faith, God is fused and confused with the individual believer, one heart at a time, and "belongs" only to those
who know and repeat the magic phrase, "Jesus is my personal Lord
and Savior." We might say that the words of Jesus of Nazareth, "It is
finished," become the mantra of the individual who has "accepted"
Jesus. The transcendence, mystery, and otherness of God are thor-
oughly diminished. The reality of life in community is narrowed to
a personal perspective: Because I am one with God, my way is the
true way and the community should fulfill my personal wishes. As a
result, the impulse of faith to respect otherness is subverted. A certain
sense of superiority may result from the notion of having a direct line
to the deity; in its extreme version, this "faith" trend becomes the

epitome of relativism under the guise of deep faithfulness. "Faith" becomes a matter of fulfilling the will of the individual under the guise of God's will. Rather than acknowledging any shared or communal norms to guide him or her, the sole authority is this "Jesus in my heart" conviction as it serves to validate and justify the individual's choices. In this option, even scripture takes a back seat to the overemphasis on personal experience, as it functions to confirm the individual's desires, often by means of a few proof-texts.

The No-Strings-Attached Option

The fourth prevalent distortion of faith, the no-strings-attached option, represents an alternative version of privatization, though it continues to place an emphasis on individual experience as normative. This option finds expression among those who wish to practice their faith without any demands being placed upon them, without any external norms imposed upon their beliefs and actions in the world. Sometimes this version of faith takes an intellectual form, in which having "faith" qualifies and justifies the individual's personal beliefs and practices, or better, lack of beliefs and practices, because the person considers his own experience and intellect as superseding that of earlier generations and contemporary believers who are less sophisticated or less mature in their thinking and experiences. In this case, the person knows best and can justify his actions.

Other times the no-strings-attached option is simply a matter of choosing to become a member of a particular church in order to receive the services and social aspects provided. As if joining the local automobile club or YMCA, in this version of "faith" the persons seek the supposed benefits of membership without accepting or acknowledging any obligations placed upon their time or resources, or at best, accepting a limited obligation in return for services rendered. Once again, much as in the "Jesus in my heart" option, church membership can be understood as a process of moving individuals toward their personal goals of success and happiness. If the community assists in this process, then the individuals contribute in some way. If the community fails to assist them toward fulfilling their personal goals, then the community is criticized and contributions are withheld. Adhering to a no-strings-attached faith is about personal fulfillment, rather than a commitment to a way of life that is wider and deeper than our individual desires. It diverts our attention away from what we most deeply long to have by faith in God: the good life and human flourishing that arise from genuine relationality.

In a variation on this no-strings-attached theme, faith is often misunderstood as the opposite of the condition of sin, and because the church as institution and Christians as human beings remain sinful, the person becomes critical of the community and isolates himself from it. This response manifests a form of self-justification in which the person understands herself as better without the community than within it. In this case, the person of "faith" fails to distinguish between religion in its institutional forms (i.e., *the* faith, in its existential, constructed form) and faith in God (as a web of relationships). The brokenness of the institutions of human life remains an inescapable part of the human condition. We cannot isolate ourselves from the Christian community if our faith is in God, because any notion of "separate and better" is antithetical to the very nature of faith and, in actuality, is simply another expression of human brokenness.

The distinction between faith and religion is a complicated one, because they are interwoven and interrelated realities. For faith to flourish and grow, we need community, and communities require some organization or structure to create continuity and to carry out the mission of the church and the proclamation of the gospel. Moreover, in a theological sense, we cannot help but be in community when we have faith in God because, by its very nature, faith establishes relationships as both a gift and a demand. Faith is a gift that restores relationships with God and others, though we must continue to grow into the fullness of relationality, learning over time how to live in community, rather than as isolated and broken-off individuals. Faith is a demand to be outwardly oriented and to embrace the otherness of God and neighbor, which means that we must participate in communities of faith and in human communities beyond the church.

Yet we recognize and, at times, are disillusioned by the fact that our institutions fall short of the reality of God, as do individual persons. Augustine of Hippo coined the oft-repeated analogy that, far from being perfect, the church is a hospital for sinners, and we participate in the life of religious institutions in order to nurture and form us in the faith, as well as to call us to accountability, just as we nurture and nourish and hold others, and the church itself, accountable. We must learn how to live in community before and with God and others; this process takes time and a concerted effort of responding to God's grace, and is a process that is riddled with missteps and mistakes. When our institutions fail to manifest the reality of God — and fail they will — then the Protestant principle, the re-forming of the church to more fully represent the Word of God, must be invoked. The reformation, to paraphrase Schleiermacher, is without end within the confines of history. Thus, we live in the uncomfortable tension of needing the life of community to facilitate our faith, but having to call that same community to accountability. It is easy to hold one's faith in private; it is difficult to exercise it within human relationships and in deference to God.

In a related manner, the no-strings-attached option can manifest itself when individuals who claim faith in Christ abandon the community of believers because they "get nothing out of it," because the sermon is a bore, the music is worn, and any spiritual high is lacking. The individual claims to "get more" out of walking in the woods, listening to music, watching a televangelist, or working at the homeless shelter once a week. But genuine faith is never about worship services being ideally suited to the needs and desires of individual members of the community, and when this claim to "getting nothing out of it" is posited, the person has misunderstood faith and worship and the relationship between them. Faith in God is about receiving and sharing grace. It carries certain expectations and obligations, but it is never about receiving a personal list of spiritual and material goods or about being entertained — though some of today's churches are high on entertainment value, such as the Texas pastor who drove a tank into the sanctuary and proceeded to preach from atop its turret. Rather, worship is the time set apart to give thanks and praise to God, whether or not we overtly "feel" or "receive" anything in return. Our *awareness* of God's actions among us is not the heart of worship. While experiences of God's presence are not to be discounted or derided and are integral to many faith communities, at times, experiences can be deceiving. Rather than focusing on our moment-to-moment feelings, the focal point of worship is always the living God. Thus, when we seek first to receive, whether in expecting a spiritual high, material prosperity, or a "good show," we blur the distinction between the gift of faith and the necessity of religion, of life together in its ongoing brokenness, and the demand for us to embrace otherness through what we offer to God and others. Our goal is to recognize what we have been given in God in Christ in the Holy Spirit and to return our praise and thanksgiving through worship and service which, in turn, facilitates our growth into the fullness of relationality, human flourishing, and the good life.

The Four Options Revisited

Having examined the four contemporary options by which we can and do compromise our faith, we recognize that these versions of "faith" do not provide an exhaustive listing, but rather characterize broadly construed approaches that find expression in myriad variations. The point is to suggest, heuristically, that in distorting the excellence of faith, whether through belief in some external authority — in the form of science and technology or the church itself as our saving graces — or through internal authority via the privatization of faith manifest as "Jesus is my personal Lord and Savior," or as an expectation of what we should receive from the church, we want faith to be a quick and easy fix for the concrete situations of our lives, producing results on demand for us as individuals and for our society. We want to believe that faith in these things will bring us the good life, moral superiority, and a certain future in the twinkling of an eye.

Yet the scriptural witnesses suggest otherwise. The great summary statement of faith, presented in Hebrews 11–12, suggests a very different understanding of faith than today's prevailing options offer us. These chapters locate faith in God both as the source and goal of faith, as well as the subject of grace. They present faith as a journey that does not lead precisely to the place of our choosing or the fulfillment of our expectations, whether individually or communally generated. Hebrews speaks of faith as a matter of living in the midst of the world as it is, in all its brokenness, by an emphasis upon acts that are life-giving and life-sustaining. Turning to the witness borne by the letter to the Hebrews, we can begin to chart our way toward a clearer understanding of what the excellence of faith is and how it shapes our life in the world toward embodying and expressing the good life.

THE CHARACTER OF FAITH IN GOD

Of the three qualities that form the excellence of human character and facilitate the embodiment of the good life, faith is the starting point. Faith is the first step, the gentle rap upon the door, the point at which the trailhead leading to the mountain's summit comes into view. Though the journey has only commenced, paradoxically, when we take the first step or enter the trail, we find ourselves already on the mountain, within the reality of faith, and open to an entirely new way of being in the world. At its core, the excellence of faith can be defined as accepting that God's will and way are in our best interest, despite rational claims, empirical data, and societal standards that might suggest otherwise. Faith, the hand of grace, is extended to us, and we are moved to take hold of that hand and trust the integrity and reality of the covenant established in that moment. Christian faith acknowledges that God is both the source and the goal of our faith, the alpha and omega of our spiritual journey.

Although on the surface, faith appears to be the easiest thing in the world, requiring nothing more than our consent to what God offers to each of us, it is, in fact, one of the most difficult gifts to accept. This is true not only because faith demands that we be outwardly oriented and embrace the otherness of God and neighbor, but also because faith requires us to trust in the unseen, to accept the Word of the witnesses, to follow a path that is often in conflict with the ways of our North American society. Faith is always a risk, or as Barbara Brown Taylor has described it, faith is crossing a deep gorge on a rope bridge.[7] The risk in choosing that path is clear, but step by step we cross to the other side, trusting the words of those who have gone before us. Or we might think of faith as diving backwards off a craggy, oceanside cliff into the open arms of God, trusting that God will not let us plunge into the dangerous waters below. We want to believe that faith is the easiest thing in the world, but faith involves risk and a willingness to embrace the uncertain certainty it entails. It is a risk upon which we are willing to bet our lives. In his famous "wager," Blaise Pascal long ago framed this risk in relation to its alternative: If we believe in God and there is no God, we lose nothing; if we do not believe in God and God exists, then we lose everything. As Christians, we believe that the risk of faith is, indeed, about our lives and well-being in an ultimate sense. We wager that placing our lives in God's hands offers us a better chance of attaining the good life than does buying into the standards and ways of the world and its broken-offness.

When we turn to the faith statement in Hebrews 11–12, many figures of faith come into sharp relief and provide us with some touchstones by which we can begin to trace the contours of the excellence of faith. This passage, in concert with other scriptural witnesses, helps us to discern, first, the nature of faith in its giftlike quality; second, the reality of faith or what it means for those who open their lives to

God's guidance and care; and third, the liberating response of faith as a demand.

The Nature of Faith as a Gift

Faith in the Unseen. Chapter 11 of the letter to the Hebrews begins with these words, long considered to represent the fundamental nature of faith: "Now faith is the assurance of things hoped for, the conviction of things not seen" (11:1). When we read this verse, we recognize that faith relates directly and unwaveringly to the unseen. The reality of God, which is deeper and wider than the immediacy of our created world, is prior to all that we can comprehend by means of our human senses and intellect. In his lectures in *Creation and Fall*, Dietrich Bonhoeffer writes of the beginning of creation as a "limit" that we cannot go beyond as human beings. That which is prior to creation, prior to human existence, cannot be grasped from the middle of existence. By nature, then, faith looks to the very edges of what can be known rationally and empirically, understanding that there is more to life than meets the eye or crosses the mind. It accepts that the brokenness of human life is not ultimate.

The letter to the Hebrews demonstrates the priority of the unseen in the lives of several figures of faith. We are told that "Noah, warned by God about events as yet unseen, respected this warning" (11:7). As an act of accepting that God's way was in his best interest, despite evidences to the contrary, Noah built the ark. We are told that, by faith in God, Abraham "set out, not knowing where he was going" (11:8). Even though he could not see the promised land, he accepted that going the way God asked was in his family's best interest. Indeed, the faithful "desire a better country," looking by faith not to the world's standards so readily grasped, but to the promises of God that arrest our attention like a faint scent carried on a soft breeze. Our ancestors in the faith have always looked to the unseen as a priority for living their lives. So, too, might we point to contemporary figures of faith — Martin Luther King Jr., Oscar Romero, Mother Teresa of Calcutta — who looked beyond the desperation of life in its brokenness, believing that by the grace and power of God they might be agents of transformation, mediators of life in the face of death. They believed in the priority of the unseen as what is most real, and they illuminated the folly of the world's destructive ways.

The priority of the unseen is central to the faith of Jesus of Nazareth, to whom we can look to deepen our understanding of the nature of faith. The temptation scene, found in Matthew 4 and Luke 4, enables us explore the parameters of the faith of Jesus. Although the Gospel writers vary in the details and the order of the three temptations, their depictions of the overarching concern, the faith of Jesus, remain the same. In this narrative, Jesus is led into the wilderness by the Spirit, where he fasts for forty days and nights, the perfect number according to scripture, and then he is confronted by the devil. Three temptations are dangled before Jesus: (1) the temptation to material possessions and physical goods or to have his personal needs met, represented by the stones becoming loaves of bread; (2) the temptation to immortality, in which he might overcome the finite limits of human existence by jumping from the temple in expectation of being rescued by angels; and (3) the temptation to power and influence over others in ruling over the kingdoms of the world. In each case, Jesus points neither toward his own needs and desires nor toward society's standards, but to God and God's Word.

If we read this narrative on the spiritual-theological level, its power and importance for the excellence of faith is illuminated. Sandwiched between the baptism of Jesus and the beginning of his ministry, the wilderness scene takes on greater significance. His baptism is not followed by a great spiritual high in which he is given all things, but rather it is a time of being in the wilderness. Metaphorically, the wilderness is often equated with periods of spiritual dryness or what the Christian mystic, Saint John of the Cross, referred to as the "dark night of the soul." The dark night of the soul is sometimes called "blind faith," because in the midst of this wilderness, there is no immediate experience of God and, in addition, the community's comfort and encouragement seem unable to break open the darkness. In the wilderness, there is no way to see or feel or hear God's presence, and often even the community of faith offers little if any comfort, because God seems so totally hidden and inaccessible. Yet the person in the midst of the wilderness continues to follow God's way by faith alone. Jesus of Nazareth thus begins his life of ministry in the wilderness, the dark night of the soul, and that is where his earthly ministry ends, on the cross, alone, abandoned, crying out for God who now seems so hidden and inaccessible.

In spite of the depths of the wilderness and the temptations before him, Jesus demonstrates two important aspects of faith. First, despite the situation, Jesus continues to rely upon the grace of God. As a spiritual discipline, fasting is a "means of grace"; it is a means by which the grace of God may be mediated to us. We can surmise that Jesus remained prayerful throughout this time of fasting. Seeking to remain attuned to God, Jesus relies upon the means of grace for the perfect length of time, forty days and nights. He is content to await grace, without putting any restrictions upon how long he will seek God or what he expects in return. Rather, in fasting, he gives himself over to God, knowing that God will work in and through him as God wills. It is, in a sense, a time of waiting on God. It is a time of simply being open and undemanding. Here we see that Jesus accepts God's will and way as being in his best interest. He seeks God, but does so on God's terms and not his own.

The second dimension of the faith of Jesus worth noting is that he points consistently to God, away from himself and his own human desires, to the way and Word of God. Each time, no matter the temptation placed before him, Jesus looks to God and directs our attention there. Again, we might suggest that this is another way of demonstrating the priority of the unseen, as difficult as it may be for us to comprehend at times, especially times when we find ourselves wandering in the wilderness, murmuring at God for having led us to this point of dryness and near-despair. The words of Jesus in the Gospel of John, "I am the way" (14:6ff), take on new meaning, as does the claim, "I am the light of the world" (John 8:12). The way that Jesus represents, the light that he shines, is that of God. He, himself, in his very being and existence, points to God and the priority of the unseen.

Thus, when we look to the faith of Jesus, we find that faith means putting God first in our lives. It is about opening ourselves to God's way and trusting that it is in our best interest, despite what our physical senses or society may tell us at any given time. Our senses, our society, as if the "devil" of the wilderness, say to us, "God's not here, worry about your hunger, your security, your power, yourself." But Jesus' own faith tells us the opposite: God is present, trust and embrace God's way, wait for God's movement and guidance. Jesus of Nazareth thus demonstrates, in no uncertain terms, that faith looks always and only to God and God's way.

Of course, some might contend that when we interpret this scene in terms of Jesus' openness, his constant reliance on God alone, and his refusal to fulfill his basic need of food, we are encouraging a damaging, even abusive, form of self-denial; however, this is far from being the case. To the contrary, Jesus of Nazareth upholds the sanctity and well-being of the person. Jesus bears witness to the flourishing of life in all that he is and does. But this concern about how to interpret his orientation toward "selflessness," or the reality of God as a priority, brings us to the second dimension of the nature of faith described in Hebrews 11–12 because, when we examine the list of faithful and their acts, several of them strike our contemporary sensibilities as dangerous, even abusive, examples to follow. There is Abraham who is willing to offer up Isaac as a sacrifice to God. There are references to those who were "tortured," "suffered mocking and flogging, and even chains and imprisonment," "stoned to death," "sawn in two," and "destitute, persecuted, tormented" (11:36–38). Here faith in God strikes us as a life-threatening and disempowering condition. What sort of gift is this when our lives are already full of sorrows and woe?

The Life-Centered Nature of Faith. If we begin by examining the life-giving quality of faith, it will move us toward clarity in understanding the very difficult figures of faith found in the letter to the Hebrews. First, we should not overlook the fact that a number of the figures in the statement of faith point us toward the fullness of life. Noah, by faith, built an ark to save his household and preserve the integrity of all living things. Sarah, by faith, furthered life in and through bearing Isaac. Abraham, by faith, was shown that God is a God of life, not death, in protecting Isaac from harm. Moses' mother, by faith, preserved his life by placing him into a basket and floating him down the Nile to where Pharaoh's daughter bathed. Indeed, the testimony to the life-giving character of faith is evident in these words:

> For time would fail me to tell of Gideon, Barak, Samson, Jephthah, of David and Samuel and the prophets — who through faith conquered kingdoms, administered justice, obtained promises, shut the mouths of lions, quenched raging fire, escaped the edge of the sword, won strength out of weakness, became mighty in war, put foreign armies to flight. Women received their dead by resurrection. (11:32–35)

If we read these verses in a spiritual-theological light, we recognize that the gist of each of these phrases demonstrates how life was furthered and enabled to flourish. Certainly, we can call into question the appropriateness of war and violence as a means of life or as God's will for us, but war and violence are an inescapable dimension of the brokenness of human society as we know it, and ending such violence is called for. Life, not death, is God's will, and by its very nature, faith is life-giving and life-promoting. We might say that faith is life-centered.

To defend this claim to the life-centered nature of faith, we can turn to the Gospels and, once again, to the faith of Jesus. The gospel, the good news, is a life-centered discourse. The proclamation of life begins with the incarnation, God assuming human flesh. In this act, God affirms the value and goodness of human life, as God cannot do anything contrary to God's nature. The infant Jesus, Emmanuel, upholds and proclaims God's promise and provision for the fullness of life. In the ministry of Jesus, life remains central. The miracles he performs bear witness that God wills the flourishing of human life: casting out demons, curing diseases, feeding the hungry, welcoming the outcast, taking children into his arms. Even the Canaanite woman of Matthew 15 is offered life, against all odds. As a woman and an enemy of Israel, she has everything working against her according to societal standards. Yet she convinces Jesus, after an initial rebuke, to heal her daughter because of the greatness of her faith. Finally, in the resurrection of Jesus Christ, God proclaims once and for all time the centrality of life. God says no to our death-dealing acts. God is a God of life, and the birth, life, and resurrection of Jesus all testify to the life-centered character of faith.

The Meaning of a Life Lived by Faith in God

The Goodness of Life as God Intended. The unseen and life-centered nature of faith forces us to return to the difficult aspects of the faith journey according to Hebrews 11–12, as well as to raise the question of the cross and the ugliness and brutality of Jesus' death. Can the fullness of life be attained only by virtue of enduring distressing, painful, and dangerous forms of suffering and death? Is this what faith in God demands? The answer is no, but a qualified no. In the beginning, God created all things and declared them good, including human life. God intends for the whole of creation to live the good life as has been proclaimed from the beginning. Indeed, when God became flesh in Jesus of Nazareth, death on the cross was not a given. Theological tradition has suggested that the atonement, the reconciliation of God and humanity, could only occur by means of the cross, whether to satisfy the justice of God or to ransom humanity from the grips of "Satan," yet the message of the incarnation implies otherwise. Feminist and Womanist theologians have stressed that the atonement, reconciliation, occurs in the union of God and humanity in Jesus of Nazareth and in his ability to resist the three temptations in the wilderness. Long before Jesus said, "This is my body given for you," at the Last Supper with the disciples, God announced, "This is my body given for you: this helpless, vulnerable baby. Love me. Care for me. Uphold my life." Yet humanity continued to turn a deaf ear on the Word and the way of God, pointing fingers and shoving Jesus to the cross. The brokenness of human nature raised up death and taunted the reality of the good life as proclaimed by God in the flesh, preferring its own misguided ways. Even so, God had the last word: The promise of life in its fullness; the goodness proclaimed in the beginning, in the resurrection, and in the promised future.

The Brokenness of Life in Human Community. Like Jesus of Nazareth, we, too, are confronted with the inescapable brokenness of the world and human communities. We cannot escape from this world, even as we are incorporated into the reality of God. Faith cannot be viewed as a magic potion; we cannot click together the heels of our ruby-red slippers and find ourselves instantly transported to the "better country" for which our hearts yearn. Thus, in spite of and, at times, because of our faith in God and our concomitant rejection of society's standards, we suffer painful, unjust, and undesired circumstances, not at the hands of God, but by our own human hands, especially those hands that refuse, even now, to heed and uphold God's life-giving Word.

This reality is central to the faith statement of the letter to the Hebrews. In it, we find that faith in God neither leads us to a life filled with all the things we might want and desire nor removes us from life on earth. In fact, we might say that it sends us back into the world in all its messiness to be agents of transformation, helping to liberate people to the fullness of life. Faith does not enable us to escape from the world, but rather provides the means to endure it and to attend to its renewal by the grace and power of God in Christ in the Holy Spirit. Faith opens our "spiritual senses" to the reality and presence of God with and among us, strengthening and guiding our actions. Moreover, as Hebrews makes clear, the movement of faith in the world will not always be valued by society and, indeed, may be despised. This response was one that Jesus often encountered; it is the response that the faithful might receive in this day and age, especially if they are living out the reality of faith in God and not a misplaced faith. God's way is always a threat to what broken nature holds dear and covets as the "good life."

Faith as a Process. Finally, the meaning of faith in God must always be understood, from a historical, temporal perspective, as a process in which our faith can and does grow. Faith is not a static state, but a dynamic process. Sometimes gradual, sometimes startling in its swiftness, faith is always on the move, and the more we accept and exercise faith in God, the more faith we have and exercise. Genuine trust comes only through trusting, and grows over time. We see this process of growth, for example, in the transformation of Moses from a man who had fallen from power in Pharaoh's courts after murdering an Egyptian, hidden out in the desert, and reluctantly accepted God's call to return to Egypt into a man of great faith who embodied the power of God and led the Hebrew people out of slavery, then increasingly upheld God's way throughout the rest of his lifetime. Another example is found in John Wesley, the founder of Methodism, who is known to have journeyed by stages from expressing his faith largely in terms of an intellectual assent, to living out a faith that permeated his heart and mind and led him to spend his life working on behalf of the poor, sick, and neglected. Indeed, most people who stay on the journey of faith in God will recognize, in their own lives, this maturing and deepening process.

In the Gospel of John, Nicodemus provides a subtle but powerful example of the maturing and deepening of faith over time. He first appears in John 3:1–15 when he approaches Jesus "by night" because he is a Pharisee and does not want anyone to see him. Nicodemus is curious about the faith to which Jesus testifies, and he questions how a person can "be born after having grown old" (3:4). Clearly, on this occasion, he must already possess some iota of faith, not only because he comes to Jesus in a state of searching, but also because he is a man who has spent his life seeking God by means of the law. Faith whispers to Nicodemus, yet he is afraid of what society and his peers will think.

Jesus points Nicodemus toward the unseen, which is grasped by faith, rather than the visible, which can only help to point us toward that reality. Jesus attempts to reorient Nicodemus's vision and life.

When Nicodemus reappears in John 7:45–52, a change in his faith can be detected. In broad daylight, Jesus is confronted by the chief priests and Pharisees who have sought to have him arrested. They raise the question: "Has any one of the authorities or of the Pharisees believed in him?" (7:48). Nicodemus then comes to Jesus' defense, short of taking the bold step of answering the question in the affirmative, but nonetheless taking a risk of faith. He uses the law to Jesus' advantage, suggesting it demands that a person be given a proper hearing prior to being judged. We can almost see the furrowed brows on his fellow Pharisees as they ask Nicodemus, "Surely you are not also from Galilee, are you?" In other words, Nicodemus's loyalty has now been questioned publicly. Is he loyal to Jesus or to the Pharisees?

Finally, a far deeper and more public expression of faith is found at the end of the Gospel when Nicodemus accompanies Joseph of Arimathea, a "secret" disciple, to prepare Jesus' body for burial (John 19:38–40). Nicodemus arrives carrying "a mixture of myrrh and aloes, weighing about a hundred pounds" (19:39). This man who first came to Jesus under the cover of darkness now struggles under this heavy burden, which cannot possibly be hidden. Perhaps he could claim that they were simply fulfilling the burial customs as required by the law. Nonetheless, Nicodemus is now willing to risk having his loyalties publicly displayed. Although we do not meet Nicodemus again, we can only imagine that his faith would continue to grow, and he would, perhaps, take the risk of becoming one of the small but growing band who followed the way of Jesus. The fact that he has moved from questioning, to defending, to acting on behalf of Jesus is a pattern that suggests the boldness and fullness of his faith is growing by degrees.

The Liberating Demand of Faith

The story of Nicodemus, which concludes with his expression of faith in Jesus through an outward and public action, helps us to see that faith is not merely intellectual or verbal assent, nor is it simply an uplifting feeling; rather, faith takes shape in the life we live in the world. It takes on form and flesh in and through us. We might say that faith is a gerund: believing or having faith is a restless, vibrant reality of living out, in, and by the grace of God. As something that grows when nourished, faith is a living thing, and when we accept the gift, we also accept the demand to be outwardly oriented toward God and others. Because faith restores relationality and enables the possibility of the fullness of relationship, the appropriate response includes expressions of thanksgiving and an attitude of sharing our good fortune. Faith liberates us to a life of sharing liberation with others.

The Liberating Power of Faith as Spiritual Transformation. Faith can be understood as a power or energy that works by grace to liberate us from the brokenness of our human existence, even as we remain embedded within it. In other words, as Christians, faith enables us to participate in the reality of the living God as a present condition, but we do so within the brokenness of human existence. Rather than living only in the midst of the broken-offness of self-centered existence, by faith we now live in the "already but not yet" spoken of by the Apostle Paul. The realm of God is begun, but not yet completed. Traditionally, Christians have spoken of this liberating power as justification by faith or the moment at which the righteous Judge declares us innocent, even though we deserve to be convicted and sentenced. For no reason of our own making or merit, when we accept that God's way is in our best interest, we are forgiven by the mysterious grace of God. We do not deserve or merit that pardoning power, yet God freely chooses to restore us to relationship. Although justification and the restoration of relationality remain unavailable to the physical senses, we nonetheless believe that a fundamental transformation takes place. Faith in God thus liberates us from our proclivity to be isolated, self-justifying, and self-concerned people. It liberates us from ourselves by reestablishing genuine relationality and enabling or empowering us to start living out God's way in the world.

Because justification by faith reestablishes relationship, it marks a liberating transition from a life that is self-focused to one that respects and responds to the other, whether God or neighbor. We might suggest, to use more traditional language, this form of liberation involves spiritual transformation because, by definition, spirituality is about our relationship to God and how we embody that relationship. It marks a liberating transition from trusting in external authorities such as science and technology, money, or institutions and from placing our faith in ourselves and our personal power, wealth, or wisdom. It is a mark of accepting that God's way opens us to the possibility of embodying the good life in which genuine human flourishing and the flourishing of the whole of creation are realized.

At this point of justification, by virtue of our faith in Jesus Christ, the faith of Jesus begins to take shape within us. Another way of expressing this transition is by reference to the Christ-character within us as it starts to take form and to enliven us. It is, however, only the beginning of that formation in which the fullness of our humanity is recovered and comes to be expressed. In this sense, the onset of faith also represents the point at which what is traditionally known as "sanctification" begins. Sanctification is understood as the ongoing, continuous process by which the power and presence of sin — our denial and neglect of God's grace — is rooted out of our very being and we are increasingly filled with the richness of God's own love. Thus, we might say that faith is a power that liberates us from our selfishness and isolation from God and others, restoring the synapses that spark and generate genuine relationality, and initiating a long process of formation in which the Christ-character takes shape in our lives.

Spiritually, justification by faith continues over our lifetime, in the sense that whenever we momentarily find ourselves returning to the ways of broken-offness from God and others — to self-justifying and self-centered actions — then we must again acknowledge that God's way is in our best interest and open ourselves to the reality of faith and its demand to live otherwise. The gift of faith comes with the demand that we live our lives differently, as people for whom the unseen and life-centered nature of faith in God takes priority. The demand to follow God's way inevitably remains in tension with our broken, but graciously forgiven, human nature and will. The seduction of self-centeredness ceaselessly pulls against and seeks to deny and denigrate God's way as primary. This tension means that the point of justification by faith begins a long and difficult process in which we acknowledge and become increasingly aware that worldly treasures and pleasures and standards of success — that is, society's notion of the "good life" — continue to attract us like metal to a magnet, even as we pull away and strain to run the race guided by faith in God.

The Liberating Response of Faith as Material Transformation. When we accept that God's way is in our best interest and can lead us toward the good life we seek, then we must also accept that faith involves a fundamental reorientation of our lives toward God and others and away from ourselves as the center of the universe and as deserving whatever we desire. If the mark of justification is the restoration of relationship with God and others, at least in initial and fragmentary fashion, then faith, by necessity, includes the demand that we live our lives seeking to deepen and expand those connections. We must constantly ask for and accept forgiveness when we discover ourselves returning to the broken-offness of life apart from faith in God. But beyond this imperative to know ourselves as God knows us — that is, to be conscious and honest about where we are placing our trust and security — we find the imperative to extend liberation in response to the gift that we, ourselves, have received. Faith demands that we follow God's way, not only in word, but also in action; not only in terms of the personal benefit of spiritual liberation, but also in terms of the greater good, which includes material liberation and well-being. The web of relationships that constitutes our fundamental reality as creatures of God is embodied in physical, material forms that demand our involvement and participation.

To understand the liberating response of faith as this demand to extend liberation through and into the variety of relational networks that compose our existence, we can turn to the words of Genesis, "In the beginning, God created the heavens and the earth." God, as creator of the material world in which we live and move and have our being, is connected to the whole of creation. There is not one cell or atom or particle of physical existence that is separate from the reality and care of God. Though it is difficult, at times, for us to comprehend God's intimacy with the whole of creation, the reality is that God envisioned and chose to weave together this web of life in all its beauty, complexity, grandeur, and minutia. Even more significant, from the perspective of faith, is the responsibility given to human beings as caretakers, on behalf of God, for this sphere we inhabit. Turning again to the first Genesis creation narrative, we find that God blessed the male and female, the two created in God's own image, and commanded them to exercise "dominion" (1:28). Today, of course, we realize that we have used and abused the created world and other creatures, including other human beings, to personal advantage, instead of accepting responsibility for the kind of careful stewardship that enables life to flourish as a single, holistic community. Thus, when, by faith, we accept that God's way is in our best interest and receive the gift of spiritual liberation, we are restored to this commitment and responsibility to act as co-caretakers with God of the material world.

Because of the brokenness of our existence, however, responsible care now requires more than simply tending to the earth, as a gardener to a bed of neatly planted tulips. To extend the metaphor, the bed has become a dumping ground for refuse, the soil depleted from overuse, and adjacent to it, the homeless have erected a shantytown out of cardboard boxes, digging through the refuse for scraps of clothing or an edible morsel discarded by the privileged. Our neglect has grown so great over so many centuries, we must now act in restorative, healing, and transforming ways. Sometimes our actions require us, if we are privileged, to settle for a smaller share of the finite material of this earth. Indeed, the life and ministry of Jesus of Nazareth suggests to us that the one who lives by faith in God must act to bring material liberation to a damaged and hurting world. Too often the gift of faith is understood as spiritual liberation only, but unless we also begin to live out the restoration to relationality we receive with that gift, our faith has turned aside from God's way. God's way in the world requires us to be outwardly oriented to God, others, and the whole of creation in all its interconnectedness. We must learn again to see the detail and intricacy of the web into which all forms of life are woven and to act accordingly.

This liberating response of faith, faith that is active in the world, is what the author of James suggests in chapter 2 of his letter. It begins, first, with a warning against showing a preference for the rich and well-dressed, because God has "chosen the poor" to receive the promises (2:5). Caring for the less fortunate and extending the hand of grace is and has always been a basic response of faith. Then James argues that it is impossible to claim we have faith, if we do not have any works to accompany it. "If a brother or sister is naked and lacks daily food, and one of you says to them, 'Go in peace; keep warm and eat your fill,' and yet you do not supply their bodily needs, what is the good of that? So faith, by itself, if it has no works, is dead" (2:15–17). These verses do not speak of "works-righteousness" — that is, the notion that we are justified by our deeds. Rather, it suggests that a living faith in God in Christ in the Holy Spirit responds with works of liberation and transformation.

Living faith cannot help but respond with works of liberation and transformation. Our actions are a sign or mark of living faith. On the other hand, misguided and distorted faith can only speak of liberation; indeed, at times, it protests and argues that faith means spiritual liberation and has no material component. Yet the nature of faith with its life-centered focus seeks transformation. It seeks to feed, clothe, heal, and give voice to those who are hungry, naked, sick, and silenced. It seeks to root out the places of suffering and injustice as God's own hands, heart, skin, and voice in the world. Matthew 25 indicates to us that at the end of the long journey of faith, the liberating response will be taken into account. We might say that Christ will ask each of us, "What have you done with the gift of faith which I gave to you? How has it healed? How has it liberated? How has it given life?" God knows that those without faith will continue to care for their own material gain, but those who accept the gift of faith have the responsibility for upholding and nurturing God's world, knowing that our best interest is found in the flourishing of all.

Even so, we cannot forget that people who have faith in God may also be found among those who are most in need of physical, material liberation. The gift of spiritual liberation does help them to endure the circumstances of their life, and they, too, can respond in small ways to help others even less fortunate. But here the liberating response is often quite different from the response expected of those who have wealth, power, and social standing. From the perspective of the poor and marginalized, the liberating response of faith is one that calls the society and its ways to accountability. The poor and marginalized themselves must realize that spiritual liberation alone is not God's way in the world, but physical and material liberation is demanded. To follow God's way means to put a public face on faith and to seek justice. The disenfranchised should encourage and help one another to vote in every election, local and national, to bring their collective voice into the public sphere. The disenfranchised should encourage and help their youth to receive an education and to seek life in every possible way. But clearly, without the liberating response of faith by those who are financially, politically, and socially powerful, without them accepting God's way and extending God's own care to those who have the least — and even relinquishing what they have so that others may flourish — the poor and disenfranchised will continue to bear disproportionately the brokenness of this world. The privileged must open spaces in the world where those who have not been given the opportunities that money and power provide can find strength and flourish, physically and materially. The privileged must love their neighbors as they love themselves, not simply in spiritual terms, but especially in material ways. Faith in God in Christ in the Holy Spirit demands that we live our lives accepting that God's way is in our best interest, even when the standards of society claim otherwise. Either we live as people whose faith seeks to make liberation real in the world or we succumb to lesser forms of faith. Even so, a deep and living faith in God is insufficient to bring us to the fullness of human flourishing and the good life, for hope and love must also be present and nurtured. As such, with the onset of faith, we can now turn to the excellence of hope and its role in bringing the good life to reality.

Chapter Four

HOPE IN GOD

The second excellence that forms the Christ-character in us, hope, is the most difficult and elusive of the three ties that bind us to God and one another. What does hope do or what purpose does it serve? How can we hope for the good life in the face of such overwhelming evil and suffering? Why hope? Usually, we have little trouble grasping the importance of faith and love in the Christian life, but hope seems vague and illusory. It is hard to define and harder still to sustain. Nevertheless, as we argue in the course of this chapter, the excellence of hope is no less important to our Christian journey than are faith and love. Our investigation into the character of hope in God begins by tracing the contours of hopelessness and the structures or principles that shape our perception of contemporary life — structures that bear the tattered imprint of modernity.

THE CONTOURS OF HOPELESSNESS

In the midst of writing this chapter, wars and rumors of war saturate the national psyche, raising the levels of anxiety and depression in many persons, young and old alike. The U.S. economy continues to sputter along, leaving millions of unemployed Americans in its wake, depleting their savings and benefits, and rendering them powerless to ensure a decent standard of living for themselves and their families. Senior citizens find themselves forced to choose between purchasing food or life-sustaining medications. Children attend schools with few qualified teachers but metal detectors at every door. Anthrax, small-pox, black mold, carcinogens, food recalls, snipers, airplane crashes, nuclear threats, skyrocketing insurance rates, global warming: the list of perils seems endless and growing. At times, hopelessness seems to surround us like the air we breathe. No matter how healthy, wealthy, or wise we may be at any given moment, the world and its broken-ness catapults toward us, reminding us that we are not immune to the dangers, the moral and natural evils that permeate the web of life as we know it. The face of hopelessness is etched upon the landscape of our lives, even as we struggle to hope.

Of course, our lives are not utterly blanketed in hopelessness, and the turbulent times that we face at one particular point or era in his-tory will no doubt recede into the past and be replaced by a period of relative tranquility and prosperity. Optimism replaces pessimism, and fulfillment of our dreams and desires appears close at hand. When the money flows, we are convinced there is nothing we cannot do or have. At any given time, some of us travel blithely through our wak-ing hours, virtually unscathed by the hopelessness that clings to others like Saran Wrap. In these cycles of despair and optimism, gnawing fear and blissful ignorance, we recognize that permanent peace and security elude us. The optimistic peaks cannot be sustained, no mat-ter how hard we work, pray, or keep the faith. For many North Americans, finding a basis for hope and sustaining it across the dis-tance of a lifetime is becoming an ever more difficult task. Something about the contemporary landscape renders hope impotent, illogical, and illusory.

The following topography sketches this landscape as it is shaped by the three basic structures of time, space, and culture. These structures fashion our experience of the world and the immediate context within which we struggle to find threads of hope.[1] This approach helps bring into sharper focus the contours or manifestations of hopelessness in contemporary North America. Briefly, hopelessness can take three forms that locate hope in the world, rather than in God and God's promises. First, it can manifest itself in the form of rationality, in which we clutch the modern assumptions to our bosom and argue, logically, that if we can hold on long enough, our human efforts will find the answers to life's problems and bring us to the good life. Our best "hope" is found in science, technology, and the advancement of knowledge. Second, hopelessness can take the form of cynicism, in which we simply do not believe that there is reason to hope, or we convince ourselves that good and evil are all in our minds. In this case, our best "hope" is to seek fulfillment in the here and now. Finally, hopelessness can take the shape of despair, bringing us to the point where we are immobilized, caring little, if at all, about what happens around us, and placing little stock in a better future. The point or meaning of life escapes us, and the best we can "hope" for is to make it through from one day or one hour to the next.

THE LANDSCAPE OF OUR LIVES

The complex and fragile structures of the contemporary landscape are unlike those of any other era in the history of human life for the rapidity of change and the proliferation of knowledge. The earth contracts; the horizon expands; and the immediacy and immanence of our world sweeps God to the edges of the landscape, to a decaying district or a suburb in decline: close enough to call upon, but not in the thick of our lives or at the center of our activities. Modern Protestant theologians astutely recognized how nineteenth-century liberal theology contributed to the marginalization of God, the privatization of religion, and the tendency to place the human being at the center of existence. Beginning with Karl Barth's rejection of the anthropological starting point for theology and his proposal that theology begins with the revelation of God through the Word, the problem of God and God's marginalization were propelled to the forefront of theological inquiry.[2] Even so, Barth and other neoorthodox theologians could not anticipate that their approach would also ultimately contribute to placing God at the distant edges of our lives, not only by making God an unapproachable "Wholly Other," but also by virtue of the modern assumptions embedded within their work.[3] Today, those assumptions have tumbled and fallen like leaves in late November, dragging down hope in their wake. In general terms, we can suggest that the central assumptions of modernity include the belief in progress toward a utopian future; the notion of the Cartesian self or the autonomous, free subject; and the privileging of reason and scientific knowledge. All three of these assumptions have been driven and, now, debilitated by the exponential growth in knowledge and technology over the past century.

The problem of how emerging knowledge and technologies of the twentieth century influenced our understanding, assumptions, and way of being in the world cannot be ignored, for as Christians we live in the world as it exists at any given point in history. Assumptions about the exercise of reason, the nature of the self and autonomy, and the possibility of perfecting the human subject and society have been premised upon scientific achievement and empirical validation, as modernity placed great stock in the human potential to produce incremental progress toward the good. Today, however, we find ourselves tangled within the nets we have woven, wrestling to speak meaningfully of hope and to ward off the demons of hopelessness that lurk nearby.

To wrestle with the question of hope, we need to understand it is not simply that our world has changed dramatically, but more importantly, it is that our vision and knowledge of life on earth have undergone a sea change. Although a multitude of influences has reshaped our understanding of the world, three are of particular importance: (1) time as a factor of compression and immediacy, (2) space as shaped by the phenomenon of global contraction and expansion, and (3) culture as a backdrop of diversity and fluidity. To these factors, we can add a principle of "acceleration," the media moment, which serves to magnify the sea changes in our environment. Together, the three structures and one accelerant shape our manner of engaging the contemporary world, including our relationship to and embodiment of the excellence of hope.

Time as a Principle of Movement

We experience time as a sense of motion, movement, change, growth, and decay. We experience time as a fleeting image of the past and as plans and dreams for the future. We experience time as passing, cyclical, too brief, pressing in upon us, and limiting our lives and choices. This sense of time as movement has long characterized the Western notion of the human journey, but the twentieth century was shaped by time in startling new ways that continue to impact our lives and our ability to hope in God. Significantly, time has become compressed, and we relate to it with a sense of immediacy and urgency that thwarts the fullness of hope.

The Compression of Time. A century ago our days were marked by the rising and setting of the sun, and in between, our hours were connected to the earth and to physical labor. We interacted constantly with the material world, in stark contrast to the life most Americans now live. At the beginning of the twentieth century, our engagement of the created order had almost a contemplative quality to it (though, admittedly, it was often harsh and taxing); today, we travel through our days at breakneck speed, barely aware of anything beyond ourselves careening along at full throttle. In the past, we wrote a letter, knowing it would be weeks before it would arrive, imagining it would be read over and over, as the handwriting and, perhaps, the scent and feel of the paper were savored. The letter might be tucked away in a chest to be reread or discovered by future generations. Today, we send an e-mail thousands of miles across the globe, receive a response in minutes, and then, with a click of our mouse, delete it irretrievably. Once we mounted a horse and rode for days to reach a nearby city, feeling the wind and weather and catching glimpses of prairie dogs, rabbits, and hawks. Today, we sit in an aisle seat in the belly of an airliner, watching sitcom reruns on the overhead screen, and a few hours later, we awaken in another country. Once we churned butter, raised our own meat and vegetables, sewed our own clothing; today, we drive to the superstore at midnight and purchase it all with a swipe of our personalized, no-monthly-fee credit card.

Time is so compressed and our expectations are so amplified that we cannot do just one thing at any one time, but instead undertake multiple tasks simultaneously. We drive the car, talk on the cell phone, and shave or apply makeup as we go. We watch television, sort through the mail, and eat the supper we picked up on the way home. We play a computer game with our children while shuffling through business papers, making notes for tomorrow's meeting. We hire people to clean our house, mow our lawn, fix our roof, change the oil in our car, file our taxes, walk our dogs, and plan our week's vacation to maximize the leisure activities. We run red lights, willing to risk our own safety and that of others, because waiting for an additional thirty seconds seems like a lifetime. We consistently drive ten or fifteen miles per hour over the speed limit, never noticing the brilliant blue sky overhead. We pick up fast food at the drive-thru windows of restaurants that pride themselves on serving each customer in less than one minute while paying their employees less than a living wage. We buy prewashed and bagged lettuce and heat-and-eat meats. We pay two dollars for a single cup of coffee, for which the coffee grower was paid a penny a pound, and drink it as we idle in the morning rush-hour traffic. Still, we do not have enough hours in the day, and time weighs heavily upon us, keeping us tossing and turning through the night. Time has become so tightly compressed that it crushes in upon us as if ready to implode.

The Immediacy of Time. Related to the compressed pace at which we now live is the immediacy of our existence. Ours is an on-demand lifestyle, and waiting is not an option. We want things now, not later, so we structure our lives in order to receive immediate response and fulfillment. We have cable television with remote controls that enable us to flip through dozens of channels per minute. We have cellular phones attached to our ears like Velcro. We shop online for clothing and have it delivered by overnight express mail. Countless credit cards and advertisements tempt us to buy now and pay later, even months after the purchase has found its way to the curb as rubbish. There is nothing that money — or future earnings — cannot buy and bring to our doorstep at any given moment. In the breathtaking speed and the instantaneous nature of our contemporary lives, hope appears as an ill-conceived alternative to the horn of plenty and the swirl of activity. Why hope when we can have? The changing face of time has led us to pursue the good life here and now in what we accomplish and accumulate. Fulfillment has become our byword.

Time and Relativity. Of course, time itself — whatever time may be in actuality — has not changed, though our perception and engagement of it has. We can point to the impact of scientific theories, knowledge, and technologies that have altered our sense of time, placing things in flux, rendering our lives more unpredictable, and severing us from the supposedly timeless and enduring truths by which we once marked and managed our ways of being and doing. In subtle ways, the insights of Einstein's special theory of relativity of 1905 and his general theory of relativity of 1915 have altered our perception of life, as it upended the concept of absolute time. It is entirely plausible that broad brushstrokes of this new understanding have become embedded in our lives and not simply in the discipline of theoretical physics. Stephen Hawking helps us to grasp the epistemological impact of the unsettling of absolute time: "In the theory of relativity there is no unique absolute time, but instead each individual has his own personal measure of time that depends on where he is and how he is moving."[4] As philosopher Jennifer Trusted notes, "We can think of our particular description of space position and time, *as given in our particular frame of reference,* as being projections of space-time; the projection is different for observers in different frames of reference."[5] In other words, Einstein indicated that time and motion are relative to a chosen frame of reference; they are not unchanging, stable structures. Thus, "relativity" implies that perspective and individual location matter.

Although few of us grasp fully the details and implications of the theory of relativity, such ideas are implicated in the way we now understand and embody reality. As the theory of relativity gained credibility and widespread acceptance, metaphysical inquiry — the speculative investigation into first principles or those things that transcend our physical and natural environments — was also beset by incredulity. Describing the unchanging, eternal structures of our existence, a stable reality beneath time and its sense of motion and change, increasingly has been viewed as a lost cause, even though people who feel threatened by ambiguity or a loss of privilege often vehemently oppose the rise of diversity and fluidity. Nonetheless, absolutes, which once provided the sense of a rather stable foundation for our lives and our faith, have been gradually eroded such that, today, it is not uncommon to find Americans for whom the only absolute is that of the individual self and what "I" hold dear and true. In this way, the specter of relativism creeps in through a side door. There is a gnawing sense that "anything goes." Although the unsettling of absolutes has opened us to new voices and new possibilities for furthering justice, liberation, and the transformation of life, with the loss of absolutes we have also experienced a profound and sometimes uncomfortable unsettling of epistemological principles. How do we validate truth in a world where everything seems to depend upon where we are and where we are headed? Pontius Pilate's question to Jesus of Nazareth strikes us with new relevance: "What is truth?" (John 18:38).

As a result of these changes, we have come to realize that our particular position, our location in the historical flow of time and space, influences our understanding. We might say that our lived experience shapes us and our view of the world. If we can no longer appeal to immutable transcendent truth or abstract absolutes, if knowledge is subject to radical revision and premised upon our particular frame of reference, then how are we to ground our truth claims? Where do we locate and sustain hope when everything appears to be in flux? The changing nature of time forces us to find new ways of negotiating the world in which we live and new ways of participating in the eternal nature of hope. It presses us toward recognition of the other and the perspective of the other. It urges us to seek some common ground where we may stand together and see that everything is not, in fact, relative.

Time and Progress. Finally, and related to time as a principle of movement, is the modern assumption of progress toward a utopian future, largely by means of science and technology. Here we encounter a form of Hegel's dialectic in which each thesis and its antithesis create a new and better synthesis or expression of human life in history. In the West, we have come to expect that over the course of history or the course of a lifetime, gradual improvements will be realized. We assume there is an inherent correlation between history and progress, between time and a better world that we could chart on X-Y axes. We need not look far, however, to see that a steady increase in the quality, justice, and happiness of life has not been realized over the past century, though quantifying this claim is elusive. For example, if the U.S. gross national product has grown over the past twenty years, can we then posit that life in the United States is better for all persons? If that increased level of prosperity has occurred at the expense of other nations, can we suggest that this is progress? If half of the people who live in the southern hemisphere now have regular access to a television, is this an improvement in the quality of life?[6] If Christian churches are in decline in the West, but bursting at the seams in the two-thirds world, is this progress? The list of questions related to the modern assumption of progress is endless, and we are forced to accept that life is not a matter of steady movement toward a utopian future. The scriptural witnesses speak of a better future, but not of a progressively realized future. Indeed, there is nothing in creation that can prevent the human will from moving in debilitating or destructive directions. When we place our hope in our human ability to make the world better, safer, happier, and more just, ultimately we will be disappointed, for the human being continues to be a mixture of created goodness and willful negligence and decline.

Space as a Principle of Location and Perspective

The Contraction of Space. Einstein's theory of relativity introduces us to the notion that where we stand, both intellectually and physically, influences our understanding and way of negotiating the world. Like time to which it is integrally related, we perceive that space has contracted over the past century, squeezing into a smaller and denser mass. Never before in the history of life on earth have we been so interrelated as a human race or so woven into the web of life that stretches across the earth. Here, echoes of chaos theory tease our sensibilities, for chaos theory suggests that a butterfly can flap its wings in Beijing and produce, through a chain of unpredictable events, hurricane-force winds in the Gulf of Mexico. The dinosaurs that died millions of years ago become the oil pumped out of the sands in Saudi Arabia that powers the cars idling on a congested freeway in Los Angeles, where a woman is giving birth in the back of a Buick one mile from the hospital. The graduate student in Philadelphia who once spent hours shuffling through library catalogue drawers filled with yellowing bibliographical cards now sits at her computer keyboard, searching the library holdings at the university in Stockholm or Peru, making an intellectual connection that leads to a medical breakthrough.

Indeed, today's technology makes it possible to conduct classes, friendships, and a vast array of human interactions in a disembodied manner. While this technology enables shut-ins and travelers to distant shores to remain in conversation with others, it also means we can learn and socialize without leaving the comfort of our own home or learning good manners and can connect with people whom we would never notice in passing. We can work at home, conducting business with faceless colleagues in Jakarta or Istanbul, while wearing our pajamas, hair uncombed, cat purring in our lap. We can pack our bag this morning and be in South Africa before the sun rises again. We try, unsuccessfully, to pretend that those whom we most fear cannot reach deep within our once safe shores and threaten our well-being and security.

As technology brings the world closer together, the growth in population and urban space also means our natural environments are shrinking. Pristine, uninhabited land grows scarce. The suburbs have suburbs, and the freeway loop bypassing the center of the city now has an outer loop to relieve its own traffic. Like tectonic plates propelling Mount Everest to even grander heights, the center of the city inches upward and a breathtaking skyline disappears into the clouds. Solitude is a luxury. Silence makes us squirm uncomfortably. The constructed environment with its constant barrage of sensory inputs, of sounds and lights, colors and aromas, overwhelms us, and the natural landscape sinks from our view. Roosters are replaced by snooze alarms. Sunsets are blocked by billboards. Nature becomes the place of our vacation, our leisure space, but not the landscape of our lives. We are largely an urbanized population, no matter our geographical location. We are submerged in a proliferation of forms and structures of our own making. Space seems to contract around us, and our eyes glaze over as we erect personal barriers, needing our "space."

The Expansion of Space. Even as the global community draws closer and our personal and natural spaces seem to narrow, there is an unmistakable expansion occurring as well. Not only does the widespread use of technology lead us to experience the smallness and density of our planet, but it also leads us to a sense of its wideness, of the increasing complexity of our lives and the overwhelming amount of information and possibilities for living. Technology places before us the vastness of the global situation in a way not previously experienced. Indeed, if we do not focus on the local environment in which we live, we can become virtually paralyzed by the magnitude of suffering in need of redemption, problems in need of solutions, possibilities requiring us to choose one path or another, and information too vast to digest even a fraction of it within one subdiscipline. As early as their first year in school, we begin helping our children to plan everything they must know and accomplish to be admitted to the college of their choice twelve years later. Our brains warn us that overload is imminent. Depression becomes epidemic. Anxiety is our constant companion. The world is too massive for any one person to negotiate; instead, we struggle to secure a small space to inhabit, as we are pulled by the powerful forces of expansion. In this fluctuating context of a constantly expanding and contracting world, where do we find or locate hope? How do we hope in ways that are large enough and small enough to encompass our experiences? The constant pressures created by this pulsating sense of space exacerbate the fluidity of location and perspective, and we react by pursuing self-preservation and personal needs. We look for a secure room of our own to inhabit in a world that closes in on us and attempts to jar us out of our safety zones.

Space and the Autonomous Self. The principle of space now functions to disrupt the modern notion of the autonomous self or the American rugged individual who exists within his own space, interacts with the world on his own terms, and needs little help to pursue the good life. While this assumption has been constructed by the dominant segment of society and should not be construed as a universal attitude, nonetheless it has had a large impact upon contemporary life and communities of faith. Since the beginning of the Enlightenment and the so-called turn to the subject by René Descartes, the individual human being has been constructed and reconstructed as an autonomous, self-contained unit. Over the centuries, communal structures, social capital, and a desire to belong and contribute to something greater than oneself have been eroded, and in this process, God has been relegated to the periphery of our self-contained existence. The self and the individual's desires and needs have moved into the center stage of American society, only to find that the upheavals in our perception of space are shaking the ground of our being. Our own two legs or our wheels no longer seem strong enough to bear us.

Indeed, in modernity and, especially, liberal and existentialist theologies, the anthropological locus of hope often took center stage and displaced our hope in God. This displacement occurred not only because we placed great faith in our human creative potential and the

idea of progress, but also because psychology and a deeper understanding of the human existential situation came to the forefront.
Paul Tillich's theology, which greatly influenced a generation of ec-
clesial leaders and communities, provides an insightful example of
the displacement of hope in God in favor of an anthropological locus
of hope.

To grasp Tillich's understanding of hope is no simple task, since
he scarcely uses the symbol in his three-volume *Systematic Theology*.
Volume 1 contains no references to hope; volume 2 describes despair
at some length without any mention of hope; and volume 3 offers
something of a disclaimer: hope is merely a subset of faith and of
limited value. He defines faith as "the state of being *grasped* by the
transcendent unity of unambiguous life."[7] The polarities of faith and
love are primary because transcendent union oscillates between faith
and love, but this transcendent unity in no way requires the participation of hope. In other words, Tillich suggests that our ultimate
concern or deepest heart's desire can be sought and found without
participating in hope.

By subsuming hope under the auspices of faith, Tillich argues,
somewhat unconvincingly, that hope "is either an element of faith
or a pre-Spiritual 'work' of the human mind."[8] Hope is little more
than wishful thinking, if elevated beyond its role as the anticipatory
quality of faith, and it simply does not play a vital role in Christian
life. Evidence of this duality of the theological virtues and the related
displacement of hope in Tillich's theology abounds. For example, the
"Spiritual Community" is described as a community of faith and a
community of love, but not a community of hope, even though it is
fragmentary and anticipatory by nature under the conditions of existence.[9] Or, in an unintentionally insightful aside, Tillich notes that
he has dealt with Christian faith and love extensively, each in a small
book (*Dynamics of Faith* and *Love, Power, and Justice*).[10] Here it is
quite possible that the triad of faith, hope, and love was reinterpreted
in terms of faith, courage, and love; his small book *The Courage to*

Be completes the traditional trilogy. Indeed, Tillich argues that the counterpoint to despair is courage, not hope.

Why Tillich breaks open and transforms hope into courage remains subject to speculation, but certainly demonstrates the presence of the modern mind-set. Perhaps his aversion to hope is a product of the existentialist milieu, the incomprehensibility of the Holocaust, and the legacy of two world wars. Perhaps it is related to Tillich's Lutheran preference for "self-sacrifice" and "self-affirmation" (i.e., justification by faith). Perhaps it is driven by a concern for the eternal now rather than an unreal, imagined eschatological future. Most likely, all of these influences are present to some degree. As a result, whether intentionally or not, Tillich diminishes hope, reinterpreting it in more palatable or meaningful terms for the modern intellectual Christian. But when hope is re-created as courage, it loses its character as participation in God. Conceived as courage, hope becomes an anthropological moral virtue, but lacks the capacity to connect us to God's grace and move us toward the good life we seek.

Although, for Tillich, the ground of courage is God, the person of courage is not presented as being particularly aware of any relationship to the divine; rather, the person "who possesses this courage does not look beyond himself to that from which he comes, but he rests in himself."[11] Apparently, the human quality of courage is part and parcel of overcoming the *psychological* condition of existential anxiety, by means of a sturdier psychological profile. Courage takes seriously the rampant radical doubt of the modern era, such that even in the state of extreme doubt in which "the God of both religious and theological language disappears," self-affirmation remains.[12] But, again, courage is not a spiritual excellence or theological virtue; for Tillich, it is "an ethical reality, . . . rooted in the whole breadth of human existence and in the structure of being itself."[13] In Tillich's "anxious" world, courage becomes an individual, ethical reality that enables us to exist without succumbing to despair. Even so, courage is not so much a quality of compassion, care, concern, or communion for and with God and others as it is a state of mind in the individual.

Tillich's displacement of hope offers us a glimpse into the modern mind-set and the importance of the autonomous, courageous individual. Even though his system does not represent the full spectrum of theological responses to modernity, it does demonstrate the rise of psychology and ethics as meaningful ways to pursue the good life in the midst of a "world come of age," to use Bonhoeffer's phrase. It helps us to see how the individual became central, while God and hope in God were relegated to the margins. Such influences continue to shape our communities of faith, even though aspects of Tillich's theology now seem dated and historical. Today, feel-good, self-help principles; popular psychology; and "I'm Okay, God's Okay" approaches to the hopelessness we face — what we might refer to as "psycho-pop-Oprah-talk" — are as likely to be proclaimed from the pulpit as is the Bible. If we hope at all, it is often framed in terms of feeling good and having the courage in the present to grab what we want out of life, here and now. Hope is swept aside as courage and self-fulfillment take center stage.

Culture as an Ordering Principle

Culture is best understood as an ordering principle: It reflects the forms and substances of our lives and projects the practices and values we prefer. Any particular cultural expression instills or inculcates what are thought to be virtues in those who participate in and belong to it. Over the last century, culture has shifted away from being viewed as a monolithic entity or a common order, often a nation-state, with distinct boundaries from other cultures. German *Kultur,* the sense of the spirit of a people, dominated the early part of the twentieth century and contributed to the rise of fascism and world-wide violence of an unprecedented magnitude and evil. Gradually, however, the notion of a unified and pure "national culture" has been called into question. Indeed, the whole notion of culture, as traditionally defined, has become suspect and endlessly scrutinized, and we recognize that no one culture or way of ordering life exists in a vacuum, free from "external" influences, and no one culture can be viewed as the "right" or "best" culture. The third significant influence shaping the theological landscape, then, is directly related to our historical legacy of culturally funded oppression and destructiveness, as well as to the nature of globalism: the rise of a cultural consciousness that forces us to keep the other in mind and to be sensitive to our human neighbors.

Cultural Consciousness. Unlike any previous era, our contemporary context has illuminated how the vast structures of oppression, arising out of competing cultures, have silenced and harmed the voices, lives, and experiences of a number of groups and individuals. The traditional "other" — that is, other than white, male, heterosexual, privileged members of Western society — began in the 1960s to claim "otherness" as a term of resistance. This opening to otherness is a positive development, a move toward furthering justice and the dignity of every person, as it recognizes, from a Christian theological perspective, that we are all created in the image of God. Nevertheless, otherness complicates the landscape and raises serious questions about how to define and articulate Christian values in a world of immense, irreducible diversity.

Otherness can be regarded, perhaps, as a development related to the rise of historical and, more recently, what we might call "cultural consciousness."[14] Not unlike the notion of historical consciousness, introduced by Wilhelm Dilthey around the turn of the twentieth century, and the role of historicity in the development of hermeneutics, our generation understands and approaches the idea of culture from a different angle. According to David Carr, Dilthey's notion of history suggests that "we are *in* history as we are *in* the world: it serves as the horizon and background for our everyday experience."[15] Culture, like history, is something we are in, something that serves as the horizon and backdrop for our experiences of the world. Culture is an interpretive position that forms us in particular practices and ways of understanding our world, ourselves, our communities, and God. As anthropologist Adam Kuper notes, culture "is essentially a matter of ideas and values, a collective cast of mind. The ideas and values, the cosmology, morality, and aesthetics, are expressed in symbols, and so — if the medium is the message — culture could be described as a symbolic system."[16] Pressing this point to its logical conclusion, culture is not only a system of symbols, but a way of life, an expression of the meaning of these symbols, which people actually inhabit — whether consciously or not. The symbolic system becomes a narrative, a story entered into, participated in, and lived out in particular ways, though not in the sense of one unified, univocal metanarrative, as modernity was inclined to posit. Culture thus involves both beliefs and practices, and rather than being a fixed and discrete symbolic system, cultures are permeable and subject to revision, as the participants contribute to shaping and re-creating the system over time and in relation to other cultures.

"Christian" Culture. What this new cultural consciousness — sometimes imprecisely regarded as "multiculturalism" — suggests is we now understand that "Christian" values are shaped and influenced by "secular" cultural factors such as ethnicity, science, class, race, gender, political commitment, education, regionalism, and in highly significant ways, institutions. Christian culture once claimed to be "countercultural," in the sense of inverting worldly standards: in the cross of Jesus the wisdom of the world becomes utter foolishness. But if Christianity cannot be viewed as a pure and bounded value system — and even in the time immediately following the death of Jesus of Nazareth it could not be seen in this way — then no claim to being countercultural can be forwarded.

Instead, Christianity is a culture, one among many and in constant negotiation and contestation with many cultures both internally and externally. Christianity, itself, can be viewed as a number of interlaced cultures, given that there is no one Christian system or narrative understood and embraced in exactly the same way by all who claim to follow Christ. We might say that culture is now understood less like H. Richard Niebuhr's classic *Christ and Culture*, which regarded Christianity and secular culture as monolithic entities — something akin to two persons seated next to each other on a sofa, in a loveseat, or in chairs at opposite ends of a room — and more like a frenzied dance with dozens of people, swirling and flowing around the dance floor. While the Christian Church may represent the reign of God on earth, we also recognize that it remains very much a part of this world and in need of restoration and reconciliation. Christianity did not drop from the skies as heaven on earth. Rather, Christianity is a constructed, symbolic system that is riddled with the inconsistencies and failings of human beings, even as it seeks to bear faithful witness to God in Christ in the Holy Spirit. Even so, Christian culture is not an entirely mythical idea, because it does have a distinctive identity, a particular symbolic system, and a basis in the reality of God.

Properly understood, Christian culture reflects a basic but fluid and dynamic set of practices and beliefs, which form believers in certain values and ways of negotiating the world. We enter into common narratives, speak with particular metaphors, perform certain ritual acts, respond in specific ways that accord with our basic beliefs about God, self, others, and the world. This understanding of culture means that within Christianity there are subsets of Christian culture in which communities of faith interlace with a host of alternative cultures, such as denominational institutions or ethnicity, to fashion different forms and symbols and story lines. At times, our interpretive positions lead us to embody certain symbols and stories and to give less expression to others. Conversely, other cultures, whether Christian or not, may contest the Christian values as they take shape in a community, even standing in direct opposition to them. We might imagine this conceptual framework as a Venn diagram with different circles representing different cultural systems, overlapping in greater and lesser ways. Or, drawing on a biblical example, we might consider this framework in light of the four Gospels, which tell the story of Jesus of Nazareth in four different ways from within the context of specific cultural concerns.

Despite the complexity of competing and complementary cultures, some very basic points of commonality do exist within Christian belief and practice, and these common metaphors, symbols, and narratives are at the heart of Christian culture, even though they find expression in various forms over time and space. The Scriptures serve as a common table around which we gather, though we may digest some texts and not others or prefer certain flavors and aromas, perhaps because we have not really sampled the whole meal laid before us or because we have certain biases. The incarnation, cross, and resurrection are basic symbols for our Christian communities, though they may be understood and expressed in different ways. Certainly, our lifelines to God — faith, hope, and love — are basic to our lives as Christians and represent common threads of our Christian culture.

In sum, the common threads that weave through our various Christian cultures form us in particular practices and values. Central to this formation are the excellences of faith, hope, and love as they become incarnate in the body of Christ in the world and form the Christ-character in us. Christian hope plays a particularly important role in today's contested, shifting, and changing cultural context, as it helps to order and shape our lives before and with God and others and enables us to find our way in a seemingly unsteady world. It is the excellence of hope that best expresses and embodies our ongoing process of seeking to bear faithful witness while we continue the journey toward the good life.

The Media Moment as an Accelerant

Time, space, and culture thus constitute the landscape of contemporary life and structure the conditions within which hope is expressed. The speed, immediacy, closeness, vastness, diversity, and fluidity of our lives are driven and amplified by what we might refer to as the "media moment." Our psyche is scripted in significant ways by the media. Since the Vietnam War first came into our living rooms live and in color, the world has increasingly become a virtual reality for many Americans. Reality is just another source of entertainment, and the media's fictitious renderings of life often serve to shape the reality that many Americans inhabit. Moreover, today's technology enables us to replay disasters over and over from every possible angle until the images of terror become etched into our psyche, serving as a graphic overlay upon our daily lives. Terror, catastrophe, and evil seem close at hand and weigh heavily on our minds. Nothing is left to the imagination. To get a rough idea of the way in which the media is reorienting our lives, we need only consider the number of hours a week that children spend watching television and compare those statistics with the number of hours spent in conversation with their parents or in school. We could also point to recent studies correlating violent behavior in adults with the extensive viewing of violent television programs as children. The media's impact is likely far more pervasive than we now comprehend, and the implications of the media moment are just now becoming discernable.

The Media and the Rational Person. The ubiquitous nature of the media has reinforced and compounded a third basic assumption of modernity: the rational, thinking person (or, in modern language, rational "Man"). Because the media has the capacity to bring the world to our doorstep, we now have access to the movement of life as never before possible. All it takes is our eyes, ears, and minds to travel through the remotest regions on earth and beyond. Our awareness of events, problems, and evils across the globe rain down upon us in torrents. We see the world in a depth and rawness that was once available only to participants in those events. Because we can see and enter into such events through the media, we are given the impression that we have the means to make reasoned judgments concerning the good life and society, with little reliance on God as an answer to our problems. We are led to believe we have a godlike view of the world and its events, and this viewpoint is dangerously deceptive. We assume we know the whole story, even as we suspect the media's "sound bites" are selective, even biased. If we are captivated by the horrors, we can stare at the images for hours on end; if we are repulsed by them, we can take a "news break" and clear our minds of the world's evils for days or even weeks. Either way, we have a false sense of our ability to control the flow of life and to make rational choices that will maximize our benefits and minimize our losses.

The Media and the Problem of Theodicy. The media moment brings us face to face with one of the most challenging and intractable theological problems of the contemporary setting: the problem of evil or theodicy. In traditional terms, the problem is posed thus: If God is good and evil exists, then God cannot be omnipotent. If God is omnipotent and evil exists, then God cannot be good. But if we hold fast to the belief in God's goodness and omnipotence, then how can we explain the existence of evil? How are we to explain, justify, and rationalize the horrors that "mature" modern human beings have inflicted upon one another? How do we justify two world wars in which weapons of mass destruction were used; the holocaust in Germany and other holocausts in Africa, Asia, and Eastern Europe, not to mention indigenous Americans; the rise of AIDS; the growing chasm between rich and poor; starvation of an unprecedented magnitude; younger and younger children murdering younger and younger children; and countless other terrors? In light of the media's ubiquity, the magnitude of evil cannot be denied or ignored.

For many theologians and followers of the Christian faith, the problem has been numbing and has rendered hope in God problematic. If God can allow such horrors to occur, then perhaps the only hope that remains is the human potential to pursue peace and a better society. Maybe, after all, Marx was right that religion is merely an opiate that keeps the oppressed masses sedated and hoping for heaven. Maybe, after all, Feuerbach and Freud were right that religion merely projects our own human wishes and desires and, thus, will inevitably conflict and lead to violence. In this milieu, the rational human being emerged as the most logical and realistic locus of hope. We could convince ourselves, as Bonhoeffer suggested, that humanity can manage equally well without resorting to God as a working hypothesis. Various modern responses to the problem of God and to the burden shouldered by human beings were articulated. The death of God movement and the theology of hope movement arose out of these basic assumptions of modernity, although they formulated their answers to the theodicy dilemma in distinct ways, with the former seeking to remove God as a working hypothesis and the latter pointing to the eschatological promises of God's coming to humanity and our mission in the meantime. But both movements have long since lost momentum and have been reworked, refashioned, and superseded by other proposals. Today, we hear little about the "theology of hope" or the "death of God," but it does not mean our contemporary understanding has resolved the theodicy problem. In fact, we might argue that the problem is as intractable as ever, particularly because, ultimately, we cannot resolve the dilemma by our own efforts. As Christians we hope for God to act and bring to completion that which is begun among us, but we live between promise and fulfillment. With Paul and the Corinthians we exclaim, *Marana tha,* "Our Lord has come," but we pray, *Maran atha,* "Our Lord, come!" (1 Cor. 16:22).

The Media's Construction of the World. In the contemporary setting, the media moment with its emphasis on the brutality of life on earth and its sound-bite projections continues to shape the rational, thinking person in a manner that displaces the reality of God and the nature of hope. The media moment distorts our view of the created world, assigning values that often do not accord with the life of faith in God in Christ in the Holy Spirit and offering such values as "reality." Indeed, some contemporary scholars have argued that today's media images and projections present a new form of thought control.[17]

Zygmunt Bauman, for example, draws upon the work of Ryszard Kapuscinski to demonstrate how the American media distorts the desperate conditions in which the world's poor are forced to live. The process involves several projections. First, the news will cover a famine in a distant land and note that "Asian tigers," the new breed of entrepreneur, have learned an "imaginative and brave way of getting things done."[18] This message suggests that, in contrast to these Asian tigers, the poor have not taken the initiative to pull themselves out of poverty. Material gain is the standard of success and the good life, and those who remain in poverty are somehow inferior or less industrious.

Then, in a second media moment, the "news is so scripted and edited as to reduce the problem of poverty and deprivation to the question of hunger alone."[19] This action downplays the scale of poverty, and the solution appears to be simply supplying food to those who are hungry. Christians and non-Christians alike are convinced that they need only donate a few cans of food to rectify the situation. Simultaneously, this second media moment conceals the complex structure of poverty, which includes not only hunger, but illiteracy, disease, homelessness, a diminished future, and so forth. It often hides the role that privileged nations have played in these interlocking systems of oppression.

Finally, the media presents the rest of the world as a place of ongoing disasters such as civil wars, murders, illicit drug trafficking, and the spread of life-threatening diseases. These foreign "spectacles" are disturbing; we comfortable Americans pray that the "foreigners" will stay far away and leave us alone. Of course, many of the desperate peoples of the world dream of going where life is more promising, but the media's message strengthens the national resolve to keep those far away in their place.[20] As a result, the United States has a narrow view of the world and a faltering ethical commitment to others at home and abroad. At best we conceive of the rest of the world as a place to visit, but not as our home or as a part of our human family. At worst, the world is constructed as a hostile place that has chosen its own path toward destruction. In either case, we hope that the world simply leaves us alone to pursue our goal of happy and prosperous lives. But the structures of time, space, and culture continue to squeeze us together with the rest of the world, as if caught in a subway car at rush hour.

The Convergence of Time, Space, Culture, and Media

Time, space, and culture, as accelerated by the media moment, converge to burden and weigh us down like leg irons, dragging us in the direction of hopelessness. It seems that God is not solving the problems of this world, and our human attempts to do so, time and again, prove to be futile. We are moved to despair or to have courage; we may argue cynically that reality is all in our minds or we may desperately clutch the modern assumptions to our bosom, believing that if we can hold on long enough, we will develop the answers to what ails us. Yet we find ourselves as immobilized as ever, if not more so, caring little about what happens around us, seldom lending a hand in assistance or raising a voice in opposition. We tape plastic over our lives with duct tape and pray that the world will leave us alone. We send emissaries across the globe to ensure the world's "wretched refuse" stays off our teeming shores. There can be little doubt that the explosive technological milieu of the twentieth century has radically altered the way we experience and negotiate the structures of existence. When we add the assumptions of modernity into the mix, we are left with a legacy of hopelessness or the burden of hoping only in ourselves.

It is precisely at this point of becoming immobilized that hope is abandoned. The lethargy of depression signals a loss of hope. The self-affirming character of courage that anchors us in the midst of an oscillating existence signals a loss of hope. But hope, by its very nature, is a dynamic and communal process that enables us to move purposely through our days toward the good life promised by God. If faith is the point at which we locate the trail that leads up the mountain and down again to the immense ocean, then hope is the momentum for the journey and the compass that guides our steps. Christian hope leads us to live our lives making particular choices and pursuing certain paths. In the midst of the structures of time, space, and culture, amplified by the media moment and exacerbated by the legacy of modernity, hope exists, if we choose to accept and participate in it.

THE CHARACTER OF HOPE IN GOD

Hope is central to our movement through life at any given time and place and within any given cultural framework. Hope is the momentum for our Christian journey and the compass we use to orient ourselves toward the mountain's summit and the ocean beyond. Hope is the shout of an experienced guide leading the way or the gentle but firm words of Jesus calling to us from a distance, urging, "Come, follow me." Hope is a sumptuous garden emerging in early spring. If faith is about accepting God's way, then hope is about moving in that direction, anticipating it leads toward the good life. In other words, hope in God reorients our direction within the structures of existence, and in so doing, empowers us to cultivate the reality of God breaking into the world and to illuminate it for others. Grounded in the nature and promises of God, our lives become symbols of the new creation, pointing toward and participating in the alternative reality of God.

The Nature of Hope as a Gift

The Nature of Hope and God's Nature. The distinctively Christian way of hoping arises out of and is premised upon who God is. Apart from God, we have no basis for hope in the face of a world that is too much with us, too filled with violence and death, too chaotic and uncontrollable. But when we begin to grasp, by faith, the character and attributes of the living God, we find reason to hope. The importance of this claim is obvious: If we are unable to create or discover the good life by means of our own abilities and efforts, then there must be something distinctive about the living God in Christ in the Holy Spirit that gives us reason to hope.

As Christians, our knowledge and understanding of God is revealed to us through the Scriptures and, in a more general sense, through the created order, though God is not captive to or constrained by the structures of existence as we know and experience them. We usually speak of God's basic nature as including those characteristics that set God apart from creation: God is infinite, eternal,

omnipotent, and omniscient. Of course, we can only discern the out-
line of these characteristics because, as finite and limited creatures,
we do not know what it means to exist apart from the structures of
life on earth. What does it mean to say that God is eternal, such that
in the divine there is no past, present, or future, but only an "eternal
now," as Paul Tillich expressed it? What does it mean to say that
God is immanent, present to each and every molecule of the created
order, and yet transcendent and in no way contained or restricted by
such space? We are held captive and limited by time and space, but
we believe that God created and continues to sustain those physical
realities, and even more, that they express God's goodness. Though
we can scarcely fathom God's nature, if we dare to hope for the fullness of a life that can address the complexities and problems of time
and space, then our faith must accept that God in Christ in the Holy
Spirit is able to renew and re-create life and the structures of existence. As limited and broken-off people, hoping in ourselves leads
inevitably toward the inescapable reality of our finitude, but hope in
God points us toward the infinite. We hope in the immensity of God's
nature that bursts open the bonds of creation. In stark contrast to the
ways of humanity and the structures of time and space, the nature of
God gives us reason to hope.

God's Promises and the Good Life. Our hope is based not only
on the nature of God, but more specifically in the promises of God,
promises that are made known to us in and through the witnesses
of the Scriptures and the community of Christians. Briefly, we can
suggest that the promises of God to humanity are concerned with the
flourishing of human life and the whole of creation. God promises to
be with us always. God promises a radically transformed future. God
promises to reconcile fully with humanity and to restore the whole of
creation that struggles under the weight of human brokenness. God
promises that death shall be no more, that the peaceable kingdom
shall reign on earth, that every tear shall be wiped away from every
eye. Above all, God promises us life in its fullness, though we must
choose to respond to God's grace, to open ourselves to accept and

embody the gift of hope that directs us toward the good life and the flourishing of creation.

These promises thus shed light on the contemporary concerns for otherness, difference, and cultural consciousness. That God embraces and encourages uniqueness and diversity is revealed to us through the complexity and variety that exist in nature and in the human species. God created the web of life in all its intricacies, and as such, we should anticipate that in the new creation, such diversity will flourish. Yet in the fullness of diversity, the new creation will possess a radical relationality that we can only imagine based upon the promises of God. The Scriptures hint at what radical relationality might look and feel like: the lion lying down with the lamb, the child playing on the adder's den, God walking in the garden beside us in the cool of the evening. These metaphors attempt to direct our attention to a different way of being. Imagine a world without nuclear weapons and AIDS, a world where the once rich and poor live side-by-side, sharing meals and swapping stories under the shady oak. Rather than a progressive realization of a better world, God promises a radical renewal and revision of the world we inhabit, though, paradoxically, it will be the same world that God created and now sustains. God promises to pull together the loose threads of our existence, to weave a magnificent tapestry out of the many different patterns, shapes, colors, and textures that sometimes seem to be so confusing and difficult to negotiate. God's promises give us hope that the future will bring to fulfillment a radical relationality in the midst of spectacular diversity.

Even so, we realize that the promises are premises upon which the Christian journey is based. We become reoriented toward the promises of God, yet we remain embedded in the broken-offness that lures us toward despair. Hope is "a sure and steadfast anchor of the soul" (Heb. 6:19), enabling us to anchor our lives in God and the promise of flourishing. It is a ship's anchor, holding the vessel in place and preventing it from drifting. Yet even as we remain moored to God, we should not understand this grounding as inertia or a lack of movement because hope is active in the world. Perhaps a better image is that of the mountain climber who is belayed by a rope that anchors him to the rock, but also to another person, thereby helping to prevent a slip or a dangerous tumble as they climb together. When we hope in God, we are anchored in a way that enables us to move more securely in the midst of life's churning waters and steep, perilous mountains. We are not left to our own devices, but are connected to God and others.

Christian hope thus finds its source and its end in God. Although, at times, we may hope to accumulate material wealth, to achieve a certain measure of success, or simply to make it through from one day to the next, such lesser hopes lead either to momentary fulfillment or to the verge of despair, but they cannot bring us to the good life. As Christians, hope bubbles up from the ground spring of the Spirit and flows ceaselessly within us as living waters, traveling toward the vast ocean that is God. Because hope finds its source and end in God only, in God's nature and promises, it is subtle, elusive, and mysterious.

The most promising place to search for this subtle presence is in the testimony of the Scriptures. In many ways, we can characterize the Bible as a book of hope because, from Genesis to Revelation, the expectation of the good life in relationship to God is of paramount importance. Yet in the Gospels, hope is rarely mentioned and finds expression in surprisingly subtle ways. The Greek noun and verb that we translate as "hope" appear in all the major writings of the New Testament except Revelation, but are seldom used in the Gospels. Of course, this fact does not imply that hope is of minor concern; rather, in the Gospels, Jesus himself is the presence and embodiment of hope. God's nature and promises assume human form in Jesus of Nazareth; they are not something that remain an abstraction beyond our ability to grasp, if only in part. The hope of a good future, the hope of being in God's presence, the hope of inhabiting the fullness of life is found in God become flesh, dwelling among us. Thus, we might suggest that the central figure of hope in the Scriptures is not the resurrection, but Jesus, in whom hope is present from the incarnation through the passion narratives and beyond to the resurrection appearances and the promised return. In the words, life, actions, and very being of Jesus we find our particular way of navigating through this world. We find the hope that invites and empowers us to stay on the journey toward the good life promised by God.

Reality and Creation. When we ground ourselves in the subtlety of hope located in the nature of God and God's promises, we encounter the question of the real or reality. Simply put, to speak of reality is to inquire into how things actually are, rather than how they appear to be. It implies distinctions between what is true and false or genuine and deceptive. As Christians, we make the claim, and stake our lives on the claim, that there is an alternative to the structures of experience: the reality of God in Christ in the Holy Spirit. This alternative reality, which embodies the only real hope for the good life, is neither divorced from nor beyond the structures of existence, but present within them, breaking them open and enabling the new creation to emerge. The reality of God, like the structures of existence, is thus experienced in concrete forms, which means the real is both relational and contextual. Edward Farley explains that the "only reality you and I know is what has come into relation with us. Reality then is a relational word, and ... We experience the real only from our standpoint, our context and place in time, and in the language familiar to us."[21] The reality of God is present within and experienced in the midst of our particular place in time and space, as well as the culture in which we live. We experience this reality in the community of faith, in the resilience of life in the face of death, in the cry of a newborn, in the comforting words of scripture.

From the perspective of faith, then, God is the primary reality, the primary source of our relationality and the context for our lives in the world. Creation, according to Dorothee Sölle, "means more than nature" because it includes an understanding of the holiness of the earth, consisting of trust, freedom, and goodness.[22] We find God's trustworthiness manifest in the orderliness and basic predictability of creation — for example, the rising and setting of the sun by which we mark our days. We observe the free movement of creation, including varying amounts of choice and the capacity for evil. We see the goodness of the Creator in the beauty and life-sustaining character of creation. What makes the diminishment of life so painful is that we sense the real possibility of flourishing. Thus, when we engage the reality of God as present in the midst of the created world and as borne by the scriptural witnesses, we find reason to hope. In the nature of God, in God's promises, and in the real as it finds expression in creation, our hope is given wings to fly through time and space.

The Meaning of a Life Lived by Hope in God

Having considered the nature of hope, we are in a better position to grasp and embody what it means to live our lives hoping in God. As with the gift of faith, receiving hope means that our lives are reoriented and our direction changes — not only once, but many times as we readjust our steps to get back on track, following after God's promise of a radically transformed life. The directions in which we once traveled now seem less exciting and less promising than the direction in which hope leads us. The directions in which we once traveled now seem fragmented, scattered, and filled with the demons of despair and a slew of false hopes set like traps to snare us. The excellence of hope in God reorients our lives as it opens possibilities before us, leads us to follow God in Christ in the Holy Spirit, and provides a presence by which we are empowered to live in between promise and fulfillment.

The Paradox of Possibility. The fact that, by nature, God is beyond and unrestricted by the structures of existence opens before us new possibilities that otherwise could not exist. When a baby is born, we cannot help but wonder and dream about the possibilities for the future of this child as she grows to express her giftedness and potential as a human being. We imagine the things she will learn, the journeys she will take, the adult she will become. We wish the best for her. Yet at the same time, we know the reality of life will often close in and diminish many of the possibilities for that child.

A child born to a life of poverty, growing up in the projects will be limited, unfairly, by societal structures. A child whose family cannot afford sufficient and nutritious food or medical insurance will often be undermined by poor health and constrained from fully benefiting within the educational system. A child who is neglected, abused, or unloved will find flourishing a struggle of massive proportions. The notion that so many of today's opportunities are merit-based simply masks the narrowing of possibilities that characterizes the lives of many children in the United States and abroad.

Like human institutions and systems of oppression, the structures of existence also function to limit and impoverish our possibilities even when we think we have all the best that society and life can offer. No matter how much health, wealth, and education we have, time will strip possibilities from our lives. The older we become, the fewer choices we have for what we can be and do. Each choice we make in life, each direction we choose closes off other options. Sooner or later, time will strip us of our health; sooner or later, our heart will cease to beat and our lungs will grow still. Similarly, no matter how much health, wealth, and education we have, the space we can inhabit is impoverished. A mere fraction of the human population will ever have the opportunity to see the summit of Mount Everest, and we simply cannot set foot on the ocean's floor. Even if we could travel every day of our lives, we would never be able to visit every country, city, river, and desert on earth. We fight over water rights. We denude the land from overuse or the extraction of ores that are deemed more precious than the surface terrain. Once we alter a space, we are hard pressed to restore it. Once the rain forest is slashed and burned for the sake of economic development, the ecosphere cannot be restored. Once the ozone layer is destroyed by spray cans and exhaust fumes, we have no means to restore it. Much of our sense of controlling the environment is illusory and, in reality, sooner or later our space will be reduced to ashes and dust. Time and space, by their very nature, work to narrow our life's possibilities.

But hope in God brings forth possibilities. The opening of possibilities should be construed neither as an expectation of progress and gradual improvement, as postulated by modernity, nor as the imminent fulfillment of our wishes and dreams. Instead, hope provides us with a means to survive, to stand, and to participate in transformation and renewal in the midst of destruction and decay. Yet hope is distinctly paradoxical in light of faith and within the world. First, our hope is wonderfully paradoxical in light of faith. When we accept that God's way is in our best interest, despite claims to the contrary, we enter a narrow path that redirects our vision and our understanding. No longer placing our hope in external authorities or in the self, we accept that faith places us on a narrow road that, in a sense, closes off certain options as unrealistic or unhealthy in light of the reality of God. We recognize, in faith, that some options are not in our best interest. Those who sense they are living the good life in the here and now find accepting the gift of faith to be decidedly uncomfortable, precisely because we are to forgo certain options. But simultaneous to the reception of faith, hope in God serves to open the horizon and to unfold new possibilities before us. The possible emerges like stars at midnight when the thin layer of cirrus dissipates.

When we speak of the possible, our attention is often directed to the words of Matthew 19:25–26, where the disciples ask Jesus who can be saved if "it is easier for a camel to go through the eye of a needle than for someone who is rich to enter the kingdom of God," and he responds, "For mortals it is impossible, but for God all things are possible." In this text, we recognize the difficulty of hoping in God when we become embedded in the hopes of the world, trying to insulate ourselves from danger and decay. Such hopes are impossible, for they rest upon the promises and presumptions of human beings. Yet this text also indicates that God is able to do any and all things, except, of course, what is contrary to God's nature. Thus, even though we believe God can do anything, we also know that God's movement in the world is consistent with the order of things created and sustained by God. Although God *could* create a new color in the rainbow or *could* reshape the moon into a cube or a diamond, God acts in ways that are consistent with the orderliness and movement of creation. So, when we claim that all things are *possible* with God, we do not mean that God will *do* any and all things. In a similar manner, hope in God does not mean that God will do all of the things for which we hope; rather, if our hope is consistent with God's will for us, then our hope will not disappoint us. Central to God's will for the human creature and the whole of creation is life in its fullness, and with the gift of life come new possibilities. Where the gift of faith closes one path, hope opens others.

Hope is also distinctly paradoxical in light of the world. All of us, even those who sense their life is rife with options, will eventually find ourselves facing struggles of one sort or another, whether physical, mental, social, or material. No one is immune from the movement of the world's broken-offness. But when our lives in the world seem to grow closest to despair and the options for our survival and well-being seem to be the most remote, hope gathers strength to push back against hopelessness. Edward Farley notes that the "most basic paradox of individual hoping is that it increases as the situation grows more desperate."[23] When we feel utterly disconnected from relationships and creation, when we sense that the structures of existence are not life-giving but hostile, then hope directs its attention to God, seeking a way out.

Womanist theologian Delores Williams illustrates how hope in God functions to "make a way out of no way."[24] Using the biblical figure of Hagar to represent the long struggle of African American women, Williams notes that in the midst of the "wilderness-experience" or a "near-destruction situation," God helps the woman to find resources that enable her continued survival and even, perhaps, resistance and transformation. Left to our own resources, the world often treats us and, especially, the poor and marginalized so harshly that we may want nothing more than to lie down in the midst of the wilderness and die. Yet hope in God provides us with eyes to see both spiritual and material resources that we had previously overlooked, resources that open a way in the wilderness. Even so, as Williams emphasizes, hope in God does not liberate us from the woes of the world, but empowers us to survive and, even more, to pursue liberation and the fullness of life in the midst of them.

The paradox of hope suggests that when life seems to narrow in a situation of near-destruction or as we leave behind the ways that led us in other directions than toward God's promises, new possibilities emerge on the horizon and beckon to us. Hope is a light shining in the darkness that cannot be overcome by the world. Hope in God in Christ in the Holy Spirit gives us the wherewithal to continue our journey in the midst of the world, moving with purpose toward the promised future. In other words, it impels us to stand up and move toward the light on the horizon.

Following after God in Christ in the Holy Spirit. When hope in God "makes a way out of no way," there is a demand to get going, to move in the direction that God would have us go. The direction of our movement as Christians, what we might speak of as our "discipleship," is framed by the simple words, "Follow me." Their significance for the excellence of hope is often overlooked because the call to follow is interpreted as a call to faith. Yet Jesus' words indicate more than merely believing that he is the way that leads to life; they tell us that we must "follow," and following is about movement and participation. By definition, the verb "to follow" means: "to go or come after (a person or other object in motion); to move behind in the same direction" and "to go forward along (a path), to keep in (a track) as one goes."[25] Here it becomes clear that the command to follow — as well as the commands to go into the world, to go to one's house, or to go wherever God in Christ in the Holy Spirit might send someone — is about movement in the same direction and along the path that Jesus Christ has gone up and down before us. Following is a reflection of the grace of God going before us, calling to us from a distance, tugging gently when we stray. Following Jesus means going out from where we have been and moving toward the promises of the good life in God.

When we follow after the reality of God, we believe God is able to bring the fullness of life into our midst, but we also hope the direction we have chosen is consistent with God's will for us. Hope always remains subtle and elusive. This is not unlike when we are climbing a mountain and the trail, at times, seems to disappear in the ground cover, or we are trying to swim toward a particular point in the ocean. We struggle to discern if we are still on track or need to readjust our heading. Throughout our lives on earth, we hope that the path we are following is headed in the direction that God would have us go, though we may, in fact, lose our way from time to time. We hope that what we desire is what God desires for us. We hope that the path we choose is the path that God chooses for us. When we hope, we stretch out every fiber of our being toward God's promise of the fullness of our humanity and radical relationality, but we recognize that our hope may, at times, become disoriented. Hope remains a process.

The Process of Hope. When we recognize that hope is a process, we are challenged to participate in God's promises across the landscape of our lives. This point can be lost when we configure hope as properly belonging to eschatology or the "last things." Although hope stretches toward the promised future, it is a gift intended to facilitate our participation in God in the present. Indeed, the future is only "real" from a human perspective, it is meaningless in terms of God's eternal nature. Although we do hope for the future fulfillment of God's promises and the fullness of the good life, hope is the grace by which we participate in and navigate toward that end. As Glenn Tinder has claimed, "The way we hope is the way we live."[26]

If we relegate hope to the last things, rather than holding it as an essential ingredient of our present participation in God, our journey sputters, and the danger of passivity — simply waiting on God to bring the good future to us — rises exponentially. As such, it is crucial that we embody hope in our lives. Hope not only empowers us to endure difficult times, but also enables us to live each day, as the world attempts to seduce us with its version of the "good life" and fulfillment. It enables us to live in light of the presence of the promises and to travel with an orientation toward the real.

The present nature of hope thus highlights that hope is and must be active; like faith, it is a gerund. When we receive the gift of hope by God's grace, we mount up with wings like eagles; we begin to run and not grow weary; we walk and do not grow faint (Isa. 40:31). The fullness of hoping in God unfolds in time, space, and culture as a process of following the way of God in Christ in the Holy Spirit, knowing that our present is not the fullness of the destination and that the world can draw us back again into its hopeless ways. The path that leads up the mountain and down again to the sea moves us to encounter and respond to new vistas and an ever-changing environment, adapting to and, at times, resisting the circumstances we encounter. Hope sustains us over rough terrain and restores us beside still waters. Hope allows us to navigate through the twists and turns of contemporary life, and it carries a liberating demand: We must bear witness to our reason for hoping.

The Liberating Demand of Hope in God

Bearing Witness to the Real. The process of hoping in God and the reality of God's nature and promises leads to the demand to bear witness or to testify to the hope that redirects our lives. Testimony is central to the Christian understanding of life in God, but it also carries a particular relationship to hope, which is, at times, overlooked. By definition, testimony is an eyewitness account of an event related to others, usually with the intent to represent the details truthfully. We bear witness with both our words and lives. As an act of truth-telling, testimony points to the real, such that for Christians, it points toward God. We thus become symbols of the new creation. As Paul Ricoeur has suggested, testimony includes both an "irruption of meaning" as it points to God, and a confession of faith that includes God's judgment on broken-offness.[27] In other words, testimony bears witness to

God's life-giving presence among us and to Christ's judgment on the ways of the world that refuse to further life. Testimony invokes both grace and law; it is a compass pointing toward God that enables us to get our bearing and to help others do the same. As we await the fulfillment of God's promises, we must bear witness to our reason for hope.

First, testimony elicits hope as it points to life as created and sustained by God: it "names God" and illuminates the "superabundance" of life in the created world. The Hegelian dialectic, which framed modern sensibilities in terms of steady improvement, closes off possibilities.[28] In contrast, testimony, with its irruption of meaning, breaks open life beyond what we can know and imagine in the midst of decay and death. In a sense, the logic of hope is "absurd" because it "interprets in a creative way the signs of the superabundance of life in spite of the evidence of death."[29] Hope in God testifies to the fullness of life in the midst of death. Hope is a wildflower growing in the median of a superhighway. It is the cry of a child during a funeral service. Significantly, as we point toward the signs of life and new possibilities, God is named as the "voice behind the voice" of our testimony.[30] Our hope points toward the absolute subject of the witness, God in Christ in the Holy Spirit; it directs our attention toward that reality.

Testimony functions, second, to cultivate freedom. If we understand ourselves as caught within the structures of existence, the hope borne by bearing witness to the reality of God expresses a new-found freedom and offers it to others. Because life is tragically limited for many people in the United States and abroad, the hope borne by testimony helps to "make a way out of no way" and to empower those who resist the unjust, even cruel ways of the world. Here we see that testimony cannot be extricated from our actions. In his *Theology of Hope*, Moltmann suggests the promise brings a mission to us: we are to engage the present in light of the future, to recognize the signs of the new creation, and to work for justice and reconciliation. In hope, we are free "for" the other, rather than seeking to be free "from" others and the created world. True freedom is not a matter of self-centeredness, but it redirects us toward radical relationality. In Ricoeur's words, "mission would thus be the ethical equivalent of hope."[31] Hope makes us free for others and free for relationship; in a sense, we embody testimony as we participate in the promise of radical relationality. The possible emerges and we demand life in the face of death, seek reconciliation in the face of broken-offness, and pursue the flourishing of all life.

Moltmann's claim that the promise involves a demand thus leads to the third function of testimony: participation in the process of liberation and transformation. Ricoeur speaks of the "poetic" as the form of discourse which aims at "conversion of the imaginary" and "stirs up the sedimented universe of conventional ideas."[32] Poetic discourse disrupts our patterns of being in the world and enables the possible to break through; it enables us to engage the alternative reality of God. When we are captivated by the images and ways of the world that surround us, we cannot grasp the alternative reality that is present; something must shake up our lives and redirect our steps. Using Ricoeur's understanding of both poetics and testimony, Rebecca Chopp writes about what she calls "the poetics of testimony." Chopp claims that the poetics of testimony has a truth-telling function that challenges the real, as we know and understand it, and enables "the possibility of the new to break in and open us to change and transformation."[33] Testimony bears witness, publicly, to both suffering and hope, seeking to retell the truth and reshape the present. Here, we should note, first, that the real as conceived by the social order must be challenged by the reality of God in Christ in the Holy Spirit. Societal assumptions must be illuminated. But testimony also means that the Christian understanding of the reality of God is constantly in need of being stirred up and reoriented; otherwise we begin to equate our limited notions and experiences of what is real with the fullness of God's reality.

Second, Chopp argues, like Moltmann, that the poetics of testimony makes a moral claim as it "summons the public space to serve those who suffer and hope, those whose voices testify to survival, those who dare to imagine and enact transformation."[34] Such testimony is borne increasingly by those who have been marginalized and silenced in the past, and a cacophony of voices now marks the landscape. We hear the testimony to God in many languages and multiple contexts, which leads to Chopp's third point: the poetics of testimony is sensitive to "diverse voices, broken language, and multiple discourses."[35] In its decidedly public role, testimony serves to reshape and reorient the public sphere and to cultivate compassion. This point is deepened by Ricoeur, who argues that these polyphonic, partial, incomplete expressions converge in God, the subject of all testimony.[36] Real hope names God. In other words, the hope of reshaping and reorienting society and cultivating compassion toward the whole of creation originates in and returns to God. In sharing what we experience of the reality of God, our witness brings to light the real.

We might say that bearing witness to our hope in God opens up the reality of radical relationality and the new creation emerging among us. Because we are given reason to hope, we are called to bear witness to that hope within us, "to make [our] defense to anyone who demands from [us] an accounting for the hope that is in [us]" (1 Pet. 3:15). Not only does our testimony begin to reshape and reorient the public space as it points toward hope in God, but it also enables us to endure, to stand in the face of the world as it pushes us toward despair and seeks to silence us. We are empowered to bear witness to God, to name and resist evil and death, and to illuminate the signs of life.

Standing as Figures of Hope. In Luke's narrative depicting the woman who had been suffering from hemorrhages for twelve years (Luke 8:42b–48), the character of hope in God comes into sharp relief and enables us to see this text — which we tend to read as a story about faith — as hopeful testimony. The woman is a figure of hope as she follows after God. The woman bears witness to us, providing an account of the hope that is in her and offered to us. The story is sandwiched within the narrative of Jesus healing the daughter of Jairus, a leader of the synagogue. Jesus is on his way to Jairus's house, with the crowds pressing in on him, when a woman suffering from hemorrhages for twelve years "came up behind him and touched the fringe of his clothes" (Luke 8:44). Jesus asks who touched him, but no one responds. He asks a second time who it is that touched him. Then the woman comes forward, trembling, and falls down before him, declaring "in the presence of all the people why she had touched him, and how she had been immediately healed" (8:47). Then Jesus says to her, "Daughter, your faith has made you well; go in peace" (8:48).

When we read this text from a spiritual-theological perspective, we are reminded that, in the Gospels, Jesus does not speak of hope, but embodies it. As such, this narrative bears witness to a woman who possesses hope, as well as faith, because she not only believes that God is able to heal her, but she also hopes that it might be consistent with God's will. This assertion is strengthened when we enter carefully into the scene. The fact that the woman shoves her way through the crowd and disciples to touch the fringe of Jesus' garment seems like a small act, but the context suggests it is quite radical. In first-century Judaism, it simply was not acceptable for a woman to be aggressive, to push her way through a crowd of men, or to touch the rabbi. Even more striking is the fact that she would have been considered "unclean" because of her hemorrhage, and unclean women were isolated from the community. In other words, the woman was likely marginalized and ostracized for twelve years as a result of her physical condition. She had been isolated from the community of believers for twelve years. Moreover, we are told that the woman had "spent all she had on physicians, [but] no one could cure her" (8:43). Undoubtedly, hopelessness had closed in upon this woman because of both her physical suffering and the realities of her cultural context and its institutions. Although the structures in which she existed differ markedly from those we face today, we can identify, nonetheless, with the way in which hopelessness had wrapped around her life because of her illness and been pulled tighter by her society.

Here, then, is a woman who has every reason to succumb to despair, but in Jesus she sees hope for restoration to health, community, and life, so she takes the radical step of following Jesus and reaching out to touch him, at the risk of rendering him unclean by the standards of the day and of incurring punishment. The woman does not sit at a distance allowing despair and suffering to immobilize her or wait for God to do something; instead, by hope she is moved to act. She believes that God knows her needs, but hope moves her to remain alert, and she springs into action when the opportunity presents itself. Through her active hoping, through her participation in God, the woman's basic needs for healing and restoration to the community are fulfilled.

Even so, in a broader sense, she certainly remained far from receiving the promised fullness of life. We are reminded that after the physical healing occurred, the woman still had to face the reality of life in first-century Israel, where the participation of women was severely restricted. We should not forget that suffering and death would still find her someday, even as she could enjoy this temporary restoration to health. She remained part of the world's brokenoffness, even as she followed Christ in faith and hope. Yet in an interesting twist, her actions undoubtedly furthered and expanded hope. The woman's testimony embodies hope for other women to stand up and reach out in a world where they are voiceless and powerless. Her testimony embodies hope for the men who witness how Jesus of Nazareth responds to her, not only healing her, but lifting her up as an example to all. Though we realize that the woman had other needs that remained unmet, we can also imagine that based upon her encounter with God's own hope in Jesus, she became a figure of hope in the world, bearing witness to the promises of God, opening new possibilities of life in others, and acting as an agent of radical relationality.

Like the woman in Luke's Gospel, we, too, are called to be figures of hope in the world, following after God as witnesses to the real. When we participate in the gift of faith, which sets our feet on the path, and the gift of hope, which provides the direction and momentum for our journey, the Christ-character begins to take shape in us. But the fullness of the Christ-character requires that we also embody the gift of God's love, for it is love that can bring us to the good life we seek. In faith and hope, we turn toward the destination of love.

Chapter Five

LOVE IN GOD

We are saturated with the language of love. Tabloids take us through each twist and turn of star-studded romances. Reality TV brings together bachelors and bachelorettes during sweeps weeks to fall in love, and out again, in the privacy of America's living rooms. We surf partners-dot-com to find a bride or groom of our happily-ever-after dreams or someone for a brief, unencumbered liaison. We marry for love, not once, but twice or even three times. We love rock 'n' roll, ice-cold beer, football, and New York. We love our cars, love to go shopping, love the USA. Yet somehow, for all this love, happiness and the good life seem to dangle just beyond our reach. Love is everywhere, but it has not changed the reality of life on earth.

In this chapter, we explore love, the third of the excellences that tie us to God and others. The multivalent quality of the word "love" is obscured, and our loves become misdirected and chaotic, rather than being centered in God and properly ordered. They lead us away from flourishing, even as we think, perhaps, we have found love at last. To reclaim love in God as integral to the Christ-character and the good life, we begin by examining the love of the world in the context of three forms of love found in the ancient Greek language, echoes of which resonate in the early Christian Scriptures. These loves are: *eros, philia,* and *agape.*

THE LOVE OF THE WORLD

In English, our use of the word "love" is fairly nondescript. We use "love" to refer to a wide range of emotions and desires, including such things as sexual love, a passion for various activities or goods, and the love we have for our children, spouse, and others whom we hold dear. It is clear, however, that when we speak of love, it conveys different meanings, depending upon the situation and the object of our love. Although the ancient Greek words for love do not correspond directly and precisely to the New Testament's language, they help us to discern the subtle distinctions implied when we speak of love. Briefly, we figure our loves in terms of *eros* as the love of creation, *philia* as the love of humanity, and *agape* as God's own love.

Eros: Love of Creation

Eros, from which we derive the word "erotic," is often spoken of pejoratively. Indeed, theologians such as Anders Nygren and Karl Barth have configured eros as diametrically opposed to agape.[1] Eros is faulted for its selfish nature, for its yearning to fulfill its own fleshly desires, often without regard for anyone or anything else. Although eros is best understood in a broader sense as "passionate yearning," the connotation of sexual love is certainly present. In Greek mythology, eros was defined in terms of ecstasy or the complete loss of self-control as a person is taken outside or above himself.[2] Here, the association with sexuality is unmistakable, and early Christianity opposed the unbounded sexuality so prevalent in the surrounding pagan culture. Even so the Greek understanding of eros was far from unanimous.

Plato and Aristotle reconfigured the concept of eros by moving away from the earlier sexual connotations, while retaining the sense of being taken above oneself. For Plato, eros elevates us beyond both the physical plane and rationality. In his *Symposium,* he suggests that, although physical beauty is the source of igniting eros, beauty actually points beyond the physical to the divine or "eternal oneness."[3] We might say that the beauty of the physical world is a symbol of the Creator, for it both points toward God and participates in the reality of God. Eros yearns for beauty itself or the good itself. Plato thus argues that humanity passionately yearns for the greatest good, which is the immortality of the soul at one with the eternal.[4]

Aristotle takes eros one step further, placing it beyond human experience, in the realm of the cosmos. In his discourse on *Metaphysics,* Aristotle holds that there is an "eternal mover" or "First Cause" that keeps everything in motion and in proper order. Today, this sense of orderliness and motion can be described in terms of the laws of nature, such as gravity, whereby objects cannot fall upwards, or the fact that the sun will rise each morning because of the earth's rotation. For Aristotle, all things are "attracted" to this source, and the inherent goodness of the First Cause holds everything together. Moreover, because the First Cause is the source of motion but is not itself moved by anything, it cannot change, and therefore its goodness must be eternal. The life of contemplation yearns toward this eternal goodness; its deepest longing or desire, its eros, is moved toward the First Mover, God, whose "essential actuality is life most good and eternal."[5] Aristotle thus concludes because God's nature is good and eternal, in God we may find the goodness we seek and an end to suffering and death. Eros is the power that moves us to yearn for and contemplate the eternal goodness of the divine, and by attracting us to God it actually takes us beyond the material plane. Yet only by means of the orderliness and motion of the material world can we see the handiwork of and yearn for God.

In summarizing the Greek understanding of eros and adapting it to our own context, we can suggest with Plato that eros is a form of love integrally connected to our senses and the physicality of the created world. Eros is a sensual passion that is ignited by the beauty of the physical world. It may be passion evoked by the voice of our beloved partner for life, the brilliant orange and red streaks of a sunset, or the scent of a forest after a rainstorm. Eros moves every cell of our being to yearn toward oneness. Yet as both Plato and Aristotle indicate, eros does not yearn for these things in themselves, but for that which lies beyond or above or within them. In fact, if our passion is satisfied by the material object, our deepest human longing cannot be fulfilled. The created world in all its beauty and orderly movement points beyond itself to God, and love in the form of eros burns within us toward the good, toward a deeper connection.

Thus, we find eros in Augustine's prayer to God: "Our hearts are restless till they rest in You." Augustine's language of passionate yearning, as well as that of Christian mystics such as Saint John of the Cross and Teresa of Avila, often borders on the erotic when talking about God as the Divine Lover or the desire for spousal union with Christ, yet their writings are considered to be deeply spiritual expressions of love. Christian eros is a passion for the living God, awakened and set aflame by the beauty and wonder of the natural world. In and of itself, eros is neither negative nor harmful. But when we express this form of love in ways that distort and misuse what is, at heart, a longing for the fullness of relationship with God and the whole of creation, we are led away from God in Christ in the Holy Spirit. Such disoriented eros leads to violence against creation, the love of earthly treasures, and unbounded sexuality.

Violence against Creation. When eros seeks an end that is less than God as the source and creator of all things, it can become manifest in harmful and destructive ways. The first distortion of eros leads toward violence against the natural world. It might be expressed as killing animals for their fur, tusks, or skin, not because we need such things for clothing to keep us warm, but because we covet the feel or look. Perhaps we simply enjoy the "sport" of hunting until the object of our desire is destroyed by our yearning. At times, we continue to enjoy such "pleasures" until a species is extinct. The distortion of eros might be evident in the overconsumption of food, traditionally known as "gluttony," in which we so enjoy the taste of certain things that we eat far more than we need to sustain our bodies. This passion for food can undermine our health and promote production systems that treat animals, as well as the laborers who grow, harvest, and process our food, cruelly and indifferently. Our passion for driving huge, high-performance vehicles requires us to draw vast amounts of precious fuels from the bowels of the earth and leaves us thirsting for more, stopping at virtually nothing to satisfy our craving. Rather than viewing ourselves as intimately connected to the whole of creation, seeing ourselves as woven into the "body of God," to use the apt metaphor of Sallie McFague, we have come to understand our natural environment as a source of pleasure and a platter spread with an endless feast. We are consumers whose hunger and thirst are insatiable because we deny the Creator and prefer that which is created, justifying our desires by claiming that God gave us the earth to subdue and consume.

The Love of Earthly Treasures. Our attitude toward creation is related to the second distortion of eros, in which we yearn for earthly treasures and strive to accumulate material possessions, traditionally known as "greed." In this case, the disorientation of eros might be recognized in the televangelist who asks the poor and infirm to send him money for his "ministry" and then purchases expensive watches, sports cars, and a mansion replete with a pair of swimming pools, while spending less than 10 percent of the donations on his "ministry." Such lavish personal spending would suggest that the man's eros is disoriented toward the love of earthly things, not toward God and the flourishing of life. Others who spend tens of thousands of dollars on clothing, jewelry, or electronic equipment, and work overtime and Sundays to pay for all of the things they "love," have lost sight of the Source in their hunger to accumulate "nice things." Even something as simple as collecting a roomful of dolls or buying books by the cartload because we are passionate about them can indicate a distortion of eros. We claim we have earned them by our hard work or that it is nothing more than a harmless hobby. Yet the more we have, the more we want, and the less fulfilling these things become. The more we have, the more we feel compelled to protect our property. The more we have, the more space we need to house our treasures and to make room for even more. But when we remember that in the Gospels Jesus tells his disciples to "travel light," it is evident that our yearning should not be for the things that weigh us down and encumber our journey. Earthly treasures rust, mold, decay, and break down. None keeps suffering and death at bay. Few provide more than a momentary pleasure or diversion before we begin to set our sights on our next acquisition, in pursuit of the good life and happiness.

Unbounded Sexuality. We need not look far to see the third way in which our eros can become disoriented. Unbounded sexuality, which is often promoted through the mass media, refers to the gift of sexuality being misused and perverted in various ways, not unlike the early Greek expressions opposed by the first Christians. In this distortion of eros, there is little regard for the humanity or the flourishing of the other. In the 1950s, television shows inevitably depicted the bedroom of married couples with twin beds, as if to imply that sexuality is not a part of a good and "wholesome" life. Today, that image is laughably unrealistic, but over the past fifty years, we have made a 180-degree revolution, sexually, and now the other extreme surrounds us, as an unbridled display of sexuality leaves virtually nothing to the imagination.

Sexuality as a gift from God is meant to be expressed between loving partners committed for life; but this gift is widely misused. The media now projects sexuality as a commodity to be bought and sold in the marketplace. Supply and demand drives sexuality. The economic rationale of "sex sells" claims that good business trumps the dignity of the human being. Thus, advertisements use scantily clad models to sell everything from shampoo to auto insurance. Some of the fastest-growing cable networks are those providing XXX-rated programming. Almost daily, "spam" e-mails offer us the latest and greatest way to increase our sexual performance with just a click of the mouse. In addition to the commodification and dehumanizing of women, minors have access to unbounded sexuality in ways never before possible. Indeed, the attitude of children toward sexuality is being misshaped by this barrage of messages. Sex is little more than a product we buy and sell in the marketplace like breakfast cereals and Barbie dolls. When eros seeks satisfaction, pleasure, and profit at the expense of the full humanity of others, sexuality is distorted and pulls us away from the good life and human flourishing. We become trapped within the world of the sensual, unable to see the beauty and goodness of the Creator or the image of God in the other.

Broken-Offness from Creation. Whether violence against nature, a passion for worldly treasures and pleasures, or the unbridled sexuality that pervades our lives, the distortion and misuse of eros reveals and reflects our broken-offness from creation and the Creator. Although we were created as part of the web of life and given the responsibility of caring for the earth, we have failed to exercise justice and compassion in relation to creation. Although the human body is gifted with beauty, we have failed to act responsibly toward the sacredness and integrity of human life. Eros, when oriented toward God, sees the reflection of God in nature and the whole of creation, and responds with a passionate yearning that returns to God. But when our eros turns inward, we love only to satisfy our own selfish desires and wishes, and eros becomes a needy and demanding love. Like quicksand it sinks us more deeply into brokenness and isolation.

Philia: Love of Others

The Greek word for love between human beings in a variety of relationships is *philia*. Unlike eros, which is concerned with the material and physical realm, philia speaks of mutual affection and care and concern for others. Philia is best configured as solidarity with other human beings and hospitality toward them, as well as genuine friendship; the basis of all lasting love is deep, tangible friendship. Yet as Martha Nussbaum explains, philia "includes many relationships that would not be classified as friendships" such as "the very strongest affective relationships that human beings form; ... [and] relationships that have a passionate sexual component."[6] The deepest expressions of human interconnectedness find expression as philia. Rather than the passionate yearning of eros, philia emphasizes "disinterested benefit, sharing, and mutuality; ... a rare kind of balance and harmony."[7] Surprisingly, most Christian theologians have given little thought to the expression of love as philia, emphasizing, instead, eros and agape, usually in dialectical tension.[8] Yet philia, properly conceived, plays a vital role in the Christian life, as it brings to the forefront the nature of human relationship. Drawn toward the image of God within each person, philia works to weave us together as one human family or a gathering of friends.

Philia and Solidarity. In ancient Greek literature, philia takes shape in the word *philanthropia,* or philanthropy, which refers to altruism and the love of humanity that engenders life. Philanthropy means more than a willingness to donate money; it is a willingness to give of ourselves. It means "laying down our lives," or the lives we have accumulated, for the sake of the well-being of all, much like the early Christian community depicted in Acts 2:44–45. Indeed, philia is of central concern because Christians are commanded to "love our neighbor," a love that finds expression in life-giving actions such as sheltering the homeless and confronting racism. Philia recognizes that we all share in the condition of brokenness, but more importantly, philia probes beneath the surface to see the image of God within each person. We might suggest that if eros points us beyond the creature, philia draws us more deeply into the goodness of our humanity and stirs up a sense of solidarity in the midst of overwhelming human diversity. Philia, expressed as solidarity, seeks the well-being of humanity.

Ada María Isasi-Díaz speaks of solidarity not as "a matter of agreeing with" others, but as a matter of recognizing that societal distinctions often mask the "interconnections that exist between oppression and privilege, between rich and poor, the oppressed and the oppressors."[9] Solidarity is thus based upon mutuality, rather than charity, as mutuality draws people into dialogue and seeks to change systems that oppress, marginalize, and limit the flourishing of others. This understanding of mutuality is amplified by Martha Nussbaum who explains that, in Aristotelian thought, philia "requires separateness and a mutual respect for separateness; it requires

mutual well-wishing for the other's own sake and, ... mutual benefiting in action, insofar as this is possible. ... "[10] As mutual respect,
solidarity listens deeply and acts in ways that empower others and
allow for self-determination and flourishing. Mutuality suggests that,
in turn, they will do the same for us. Thus, solidarity may be expressed through participating in an after-school tutoring program
for disadvantaged youth. Solidarity may find voice through learning Spanish or Cambodian in order to be in conversation with the
women who clean the building in which we work — conversation
about their lives and dreams, not about the dirt on the windowsill.
Solidarity can take flesh when we vote for social programs aimed
at reducing the costs of health insurance and medications. In multiple ways, solidarity strengthens the human family. Love of neighbor,
philia, is a process in which we work on behalf of the flourishing of
others in concrete ways. Philia is about engendering social capital:
mutuality, trust, and reciprocity.

Philia and Hospitality. In expressing solidarity and concern for
the other, philia also takes root in the Greek word for hospitality,
philoxenias, found, for example, in Hebrews 13:2, which urges, "Do
not neglect to show hospitality to strangers. ... " Such hospitality is
present in Abraham entertaining the three travelers who pass by his
tent. The woman who anoints Jesus with precious oil as he faces his
final days offers hospitality, as does Paul in collecting funds for the
saints in Jerusalem. Hospitality is expressed by the man who stops
for a family whose minivan has broken down on the side of the high-
way. Hospitality is found in women who deliver meals to the elderly
and shut-ins living in the projects. Philia, as hospitality, is an outward-
reaching love for others, including strangers. Yet if we heed the words
of Isasi-Díaz, we must recognize that hospitality is not simply about
charity or, in a manner of speaking, giving alms to the poor. Hospitality is also about breaking down the barriers constructed by human
beings that separate and divide humanity one against the other. Who
are the tax collectors, Caananites, and lepers of our day? The answer
points us toward where our hospitality must go. Hospitality responds

to the image of God in the other, seeking to build up in the face of those who would tear down or perpetuate unjust or harmful systems. Thus, philia is not a love shared exclusively among Christians, but inclusively with all of humanity, just as Christ shared God's love with and for all. Philia seeks to make and sustain connections, to weave together the web of humanity where it has been torn asunder. Unfortunately, in our contemporary society, *philia* has become misused and disoriented, often tearing the web of life into shreds like a flag exposed to the wind and weather. This distortion is particularly apparent when it appears in the form of xenophobia or as the idolatrous love of humanity.

The Xenophobic Response. The Greek word for hospitality, *philoxenias,* combines philia with the word meaning "strangers," or those who are different from us. In *philoxenias* we find the deep respect for otherness, which welcomes and embraces difference and "strangeness" from our own cultural and societal norms. Hospitality is extended to the stranger, the alien in our midst, and those whom we least understand. Yet in our contemporary society, philia, or brotherly and sisterly love, is often misinterpreted to mean the love of those who are just like us, despite the words of Jesus in the Sermon on the Mount admonishing his followers to love their enemies: "for if you love those who love you, what reward do you have? Do not even the tax collectors do the same? And if you greet only your brothers and sisters, what more are you doing than others?" (Matt. 5:46–47). The love we express for humanity as solidarity and hospitality is to be extended to all, especially those most different from us. Yet today difference is often met, not with love, but with fear and hatred or what is known as "xenophobia," fear of strangers. Xenophobia distorts philia into a closed, self-serving form of love. Rather than reaching out to embrace the other in whom God's image is reflected, we pull back like a turtle into its shell or push them away as if swatting at a wasp. Xenophobia exacerbates the broken-offness that characterizes life apart from God.

The xenophobic response of our contemporary society is not unlike generations of earlier Americans who expressed hostility toward those who were different. Interring Japanese Americans during World War II and creating "separate but equal" laws are but two examples. Even so, our borders today are becoming fortresses blanketed in barbed wire and patrolled by armed sentinels, and we propel our power to distant battlegrounds in an effort to keep at bay those whom we fear. We engage in racial profiling, willing to sacrifice our long-standing commitment to civil liberties and justice because we fear those who have come to this country from abroad, and we forget that, unless we are Native Americans, our ancestors also came here from abroad just a generation or two ago. We argue that "they" are out to get us, neglecting the role we have played in impoverishing other nations and intervening in their political processes, at times supporting brutal and dictatorial regimes who might further our national interests for a brief time. We send troops abroad in aggressive ways that are largely unlike the long history of U.S. foreign policy in which a military response has been the option of last resort. Punctuating this cavalcade of xenophobia are the religious catchphrases flowing from the mouths of senior government officials, corporate executives, and even religious leaders, professing deep faith in Christ as the justification for aggression. Their pronouncements are punctuated with phrases such as "our God" and "their god." Such speeches and actions jar us with their dissonance, as Christian solidarity and hospitality are contorted into the ugly face of xenophobia, even as "God's will" is the justification. The love of humanity, philia, embraces those who are different from us; it does not seek to destroy them in the name of God. When we hate and fear the other, we despise the image of God within them, and we undermine their well-being, as well as our own. Philia expresses solidarity and hospitality in seeking the good life and the flourishing of all people. It recognizes that we are all woven together in deeper ways than meet than eye.

The Idolatrous Love of Humanity. In contrast to the xenophobic response, there are times when we love other persons deeply and unabashedly, and while it would seem that we are expressing the fullness of philia, the reverse may actually be true. Philia is best defined in terms of the universal love of humanity, which takes form in particular circumstances. Thus, to love other persons is to love the whole of humanity by responding to the particular situations that cross our path and accompany us as we move through life in faith and hope. We may respond to our children by giving them the time and presence they need on a given morning, and later that day to the needs of a coworker or someone we pass on the street. Granted, our levels of intimacy dictate the form and shape of our response, but the same concern for the well-being and flourishing of the other person motivates our actions. Although we cannot love all persons with the same degree of proximity, we are called to love them with the same basic concern for their well-being. Jesus of Nazareth was not physically present to every person, yet he loved all with the same outreaching love. Indeed, our proximity to another person's life, both geographically and metaphorically, mediates our level of response because we are finite beings rather than God. For example, a pastor responds at a different level to a former member of her church, who now lives in another state, than she does to a current member of her congregation. A teacher's response to a child's needs changes as the student moves on to the next grade. A person who witnesses a tragedy by means of television responds differently to the event than someone who is one block from the scene. A person who lives in Texas or Arizona takes up the plight of Latino and Latina immigrants in different ways than does someone living in Maine. Proximity leads us to respond in distinct ways, yet the universal concern for the flourishing of the other person remains central.

Although there is a grain of truth in the adage that God helps those who help themselves, suggesting that we must respond to God's grace and act in certain ways in the world, it is equally true that God helps those who genuinely cannot help themselves. The epitome of this claim is the atoning gift of Jesus Christ, without whom we cannot be reconciled to God and one another. We cannot reconcile the whole of creation by our own efforts. Often, we cannot reconcile one broken relationship. As such, we must acknowledge that philia is not only universal and particular, but also preferential toward those who are powerless to help themselves. Liberation theology has been premised upon the "preferential option for the poor," but perhaps a nuanced version is more true to God's nature; that is, God's love is preferential toward the powerless, which takes into account the interlocking systems of oppression that impoverish and undermine human flourishing. We are far more likely to stop for an elderly woman whose 1992 sedan has broken down than we are for two young men whose disabled truck bears the sign, "Sam's Service Station." We are moved to assist a child or someone with a broken arm, struggling to butter a piece of bread, but less inclined to do so for a thirty-year-old who keeps dropping her knife because she's in a hurry.

Although philia is preferential in small ways, it is also preferential in larger ones. Often, we readily embrace individual acts of preferential love, but find it difficult to pursue larger social acts expressing God's preference for the powerless, perhaps because our own level of status, power, and wealth may be threatened by the mutuality of philia. Even so, properly expressed, philia is concerned with the social and communal good as it protects the interests of the poor, the widow, the orphan, and the stranger. Philia chooses the interests of the disenfranchised over those of corporate giants. Philia prefers social programs that further the quality of life for the many, rather than tax laws that increase the profits of a few. Philia is unabashedly preferential in seeking the flourishing of life as a basic concern of love for our neighbor.

When we love particular people or groups of people without holding these particular and preferential demands in tension with the universal concern for flourishing, philia becomes disoriented. The particularity of our love can be deceivingly misdirected. We may love our spouse or child so greatly that we do so to the disregard of others, or we make our spouse or child into the whole purpose and meaning of our lives. Of course, this does not imply that, in the midst of a dangerous situation, we would help a stranger before we assist our child or spouse; clearly, the proximity principle suggests otherwise. But when we assume that our world and our love is complete with one or, perhaps, a handful of people, the love to which we are called by God is severely impoverished.

Another means of emaciating philia is the claim that we love America in a way that requires treating people of other nations as lesser loves. This expression of love is in direct contradiction to the scriptural doctrine that professes God as the God of all nations and peoples. We may want God to love us more or fiercely argue that the United States is God's chosen nation, but the scriptural witnesses suggest otherwise. Failing to hold other people and nations as equal in the sight of God and integral to the human family diminishes philia. The gospel never urges us to hate those who are different from us; in fact, when the gospel uses the strong language of hate, it is in reference to leaving behind our narrow self-interested existence: "Whoever comes to me and does not hate father and mother, wife and children, brothers and sisters, yes, and even life itself, cannot be my disciple" (Luke 14:26). Self-interest is urged to give way to mutuality, trust, and reciprocity.

When our particular and preferential love is an either-or rather than a both-and love, it becomes a sign of our broken-offness, instead of our connectedness to God. It may reflect our neediness and insecurity or signify a situation of loose, tenuous bonds with those whom we profess to love the most. Indeed, when we burrow beneath the surface of the claim to "love America," we quickly realize what the statement implies: not all Americans qualify as "real" Americans, but some are "more" American than others based upon physical characteristics, social status, political commitments, or religious preferences. But any particular and preferential love that is limited to certain persons and groups and neglects the universal concern for our common humanity, in reality, is broken off from God. We set up a "god" of our own making who looks, sounds, and acts like us. We make God into our image, instead of responding to the image of God implanted within every person. When we do this, we dig ourselves deeper into the human condition of isolation and selfishness.

Broken-Offness from Humanity. Misdirected and disoriented expressions of philia lead us toward isolation, fear, and hatred, rather than into varied and unconstrained acts of solidarity and hospitality. When we turn away from the love of humanity in its fullness, we perpetuate the brokenness of the human family. Rather than allowing ourselves to be directed by God's love for humanity and manifesting it in the world as the solidarity and hospitality of Jesus Christ, we choose who is worthy and deserving of love. Rather than opening ourselves to be God's hands and heart, helping those who genuinely cannot help themselves, we reject and despise the image of God in the other and prefer our own image. The Bible becomes a mirror in which we see ourselves, but seldom the reflection of others who are also created in the image of God. We thus become scattered and fragmented individuals, clinging to certain people or groups for affirmation, allowing them to become the gods of our life, instead of accepting that God's way seeks the flourishing and well-being of all. Philia, the love of humanity, properly expressed, provides a glimpse of God's inbreaking reign among us, as we recognize and respond to the image of God in others.

Agape: God's Own Love

Of the three forms of love, the one most familiar to Christians is agape or what is, at heart, God's own love. For the Greeks, the word *agape,* was actually somewhat bland, "colorless and indefinite."[11] But in the context of the New Testament, agape takes on its deeper meaning, perhaps in an attempt to distinguish God's own love from the other forms and expressions of love — distorted or not — that were present in ancient society. Agape has ultimacy; there is no greater form of love known, available, or imaginable, though we can only grasp it in part. Agape is present at creation and awaits us at the end of history. Agape is the source and the goal of the Christian journey. In the New Testament, agape is abundantly present, always with reference to the divine, either originating in God and expressed toward humanity and creation or returned by creatures to God. Simply stated, agape is a love that is rooted in and returns to God. Because agape is God's own love, it cannot be distorted or misdirected, as is the case with eros and philia. However, we can reject agape, preferring to be left to our own devices, to elevate ourselves and our loves to godlike status. We can exercise our free will and remain as isolated, needy, demanding, self-serving individuals who crave unity and seek love on our own terms. God's own love is a creating, reconciling, and sustaining love, but we must open ourselves and choose to participate in it across our lives. Agape, as God's own love, forces us to choose what and who will be primary or central in our lives.

Agape as Ordering Our Loves. In choosing God's own love, agape serves to order our lives and loves toward the good life and the flourishing of all. Because agape is rooted in and returns to God, it can bring all forms of love and life into a harmonious whole, proper ordering, or right relationship. Grounded in agape, our eros yearns to be possessed by God rather than to possess anything. We give up the unbounded desire to possess material goods and other persons, so that we may be grasped and filled by God's own outpouring love. Grounded in agape, our philia recognizes the image of God within each person and responds in solidarity and with hospitality. Although we remain human and trapped in the broken-offness of this world, choosing to receive and respond to God's own love reconfigures our way of living and transforms us from isolated individuals into participants in the web of life, seeking to be in life-giving relationships with the whole of creation.

When we speak of our loves being "rightly ordered," this understanding need not be couched in hierarchical terms or the long-discredited notion of the "Great Chain of Being," in which God is above human beings, then mammals, reptiles, vegetables, rocks, and so forth, with each piece of creation assigned a particular place in relation to God. Instead, the ordering of loves reflects the primacy of God in all that we are and do. Among the whole of creation, the human creature is the only sliver of life that is able to choose, in greater and lesser ways, what it will become and to whom it will give its attention. Rocks and precious gems have no choice in what they become. Dogs give their undying love to anyone who cares for them, unless they have been subjected to abuse. Anteaters eat ants. Geese fly south in the winter and reverse direction in the spring. Trees drop leaves in the fall or keep them year-round, depending on the species of the tree. Only the human creature can choose what, whom, and how it loves; only the human creature can ask why; and only the human creature can devise new and increasingly dangerous and destructive ways to deal with the rest of the earth. Unless the human being, as a bundle of desires, or *nephesh,* to use the word found in the Hebrew Scriptures, accepts God's own love, which affirms what it means to be fully human and beloved, eros and philia find expression in self-serving and selfish ways. As Josef Pieper notes, Augustine's claim in *Confessions* that "my love is my weight," suggests that where our love goes, we, too, will go.[12] If our love goes toward God, our whole being is oriented in that direction.

Agape as Compassionate Love. In accepting God's own love, we find that agape is at work reconciling the world, but has not yet completed this transformation. As agape makes its home within us, it moves us toward compassion and suffering on behalf of others. Compassion, as Nussbaum notes, depends upon the quality of wonder, which directs our attention to the life and the suffering of other creatures.[13] Compassion requires a sense of mature judgment and an understanding of the relatedness of life, and should not be confused with empathy, "which involves an imaginative reconstruction of the experience of the sufferer."[14] Even so, empathy has a connection to compassion that should not be discounted entirely. In compassion, agape shares in the deep pain of the world, directing our attention to the festering wounds of others and the earth as they struggle for life. The compassion of agape means that God directs our attention toward those whose flourishing is constrained, and the quality of empathy suggests that God shares in the experience and participates in the affective dimensions of our humanity, even though we can only speak of such things by analogy. We cannot know how God "feels" or what it means to say that God "shares" our pain, anguish, sorrow, or anger. Nonetheless, God's ears and heart are turned to those who cry out from within the excruciating and exhilarating movement of life, and God is present.

In a similar way, we cannot know how another human being feels. Anyone who has ever offered a word of comfort by saying, "I know just how you feel," realizes the shallowness of the comment, whether or not the other person responded with, "No, you don't." The particular relationships and events, the unique character and giftedness of each life suggest that we cannot know exactly how someone else feels in a given situation. Does one person's grief feel like another person's? Does the joy of a child feel the same as the joy of her mother? We know that there are certain common points and similar dimensions to particular emotions; nevertheless, no two experiences are exactly the same. We cannot know precisely how another person feels, yet we can turn our ears and heart to those who experience the deep movement of life and be present to them with God's own love. Indeed, sometimes the most profound expression of agape is sitting in silence beside someone in the midst of a liminal moment or at a time when the affective dimension of being human sweeps over them with raw, jagged power. Compassion directs our attention to life and the suffering of others with the intention of being present to them with God's own love. Thus, God's own love orders our lives and our loves toward God and, subsequently, the whole of creation.

THE CHARACTER OF LOVE IN GOD

The basic framework of the three forms of love that shape and misshape our lives enables us to better comprehend the nature, meaning, and liberating demand of love as it forms the Christ-character in us. To speak of "love in God," much like faith or hope in God, is to point toward the three forms of love in harmony with one other and directed toward God as the source and goal of love. We are to love God as God loves us, above all, and to allow agape to orient our eros and philia toward seeking the well-being of every atom of the created order and the flourishing of the whole web of life. Indeed, when one atom or strand of DNA goes astray, the well-being of creation is undermined. Nothing is too remote or minuscule, too complex or imposing to be beyond the love of God. Even so, humanity, gifted with consciousness, free will, and intention must choose to harbor its loves in God. Keeping this threefold understanding of love before us, in the remaining pages of this chapter, the use of "love" is intended to resonate in terms of all three forms of love working together for the good and the good life.

The Nature of Love as Our Destination

God Is Love. The witnesses of scripture make clear to us that love and God are integrally related; so much so that the Scriptures simply say: God is love. The First Letter of John claims that, "love is from God; everyone who loves is born of God and knows God. Whoever does not love does not know God, for God is love" (1 John 4:7–8). Love is essential to the nature of God. When we seek God, the destination of our journey is nothing less than the fullness of love. God's love is the ocean that beckons to us from a distance. It is the newborn infant we hold in our hands. Love is a homing pigeon in flight; it is a poplar spreading its branches at an angle to touch the sun. In a sense, the fullness of our humanity is to live according to God's own love, which orients our life toward radical relationality and the flourishing of all things. Love creates, renews, and sustains the web of life.

Returning to our analogy of the Christian journey, if faith is finding the trailhead and hope is the path we travel, the momentum and direction for the journey that leads to the summit and beyond to the vast ocean, then our destination is love. While we travel, we catch glimpses of it, but cannot envision the whole. Sometimes we are able to see and hear, perhaps even taste, feel, and smell the destination, and the closer we get to the ocean, the more present it becomes to our senses. Throughout our journey, the ocean calls to us, patiently awaiting our arrival, but it also walks beside us as we travel. The love of God, as essential to God's nature, is like a wide and deep ocean, such that we cannot know fully the nature of love, but can only catch glimpses of it in our journey toward that destination.

Love as Radical Relationality. The incomprehensibility of God's love is related to the nature of God's being. Paul Tillich used the language of Being-itself or the Power of Being, in order to emphasize that God is not a being, even the "Supreme" being, because God as creator is the power "behind" all being. In other words, God's infinite and eternal nature is radically different from that of every other sort of being. In claiming that God is love and also that God is infinite and eternal, we thus assert that God's love is infinite and eternal. Although we can scarcely comprehend or articulate such enormous love, the reality of God's love is expressed to us largely in terms of radical relationality. Whenever and wherever humanity severs the ties with God by turning its back on grace, God continues to sustain and uphold that life. God remains radically relational. Even more pointedly, God became flesh and dwelt among us, in order that the reconciliation of all things could occur. God deigned to participate in humanity, so that we might more fully participate in God. The incarnation is an act of radical relationality. God in Christ in the Holy Spirit, the economic trinity, says to humanity that God *in se* is radically relational. God is love, and in the fullest expression of God's love toward humanity and the whole of creation, God in Christ in the Holy Spirit manifests radical relationality as the essence of love and central to the good life we seek. Radically relational love is the power of being that creates, sustains, and renews the whole of creation.

The Meaning of Love for the Christian Life

Reconciliation, Not Fusion. Because love as the destination of the Christian journey is manifest in terms of radical relationality, at times our language becomes confused as it suggests that, at the end of the journey, we will no longer be human but will become God or one with God, as if metamorphosing into the power of being. On the one hand, this understanding is visible in the contemporary tendency to speak of "my personal Lord and Savior," which projects God as dwelling within and mystically fused to the individual in the present, as if the individual believer now possesses God, who is at his or her disposal. God and the individual have become one in what we might call an immanent fusion. On the other hand, we are confronted with the competing claim that the spiritual journey leads us to overcome our finite, created nature and to be swallowed up within the divine. In this claim our language projects our future as a mystical fusion with the Creator. God and humanity will become one in what might be seen as a transcendent fusion. Either understanding of the Christian journey actually leads us away from the destination of God's love and turns us back upon ourselves, as in the beginning.

In the story of the Garden of Eden, the man and the woman choose to share the fruit of the tree in the middle of the garden, which is the only space and the only item prohibited by God. Despite the beauty, integrity, spaciousness, and life-giving quality of creation, what the man and woman desire is that iota of existence they should not in-habit and enjoy. Traditionally, the narrative has been interpreted as pointing toward the desire to become godlike, the choice of human-ity to overstep its bounds, which is where the brokenness of creation finds its origin. When we desire to become one with God, in what-ever logic or language we may use to express this desire or belief, we find ourselves standing again at the tree in the middle of the gar-den, straining to fill our hands, mouths, and lives with the one thing that is left beyond our reach. Our journey is not to become God, but to be restored to our full humanity as God intended and to accept that human beings are limited by nature. We are not destined to be-come the ocean, but to sit at its edge, listening to the voice of the waves, resting on the warm, sandy shoreline, feeding on the gifts it brings to us, and occasionally swimming in the midst of its power and beauty. We are sustained by the ocean and participate in the life it brings to us, but we cannot simply melt like an iceberg into the foamy waves.

The meaning of love for the Christian journey thus begins with the reality of reconciliation, rather than some notion of mystical fusion with God. The human situation is characterized by broken-offness — a state that is inherently self-serving and lacking in genuine relationality. Love, along with faith and hope, serves as a lifeline or umbilical cord connecting us to the divine, enabling us to grow into the fullness of God's love for and with us, such that God's own love overflows in various ways to other human beings and the created world. Love's radical relationality reweaves the broken threads in each of us, as well as between us and the whole of creation. Reconciliation means the radical transformation of all things from broken-offness to relationship.

Reconciliation and Forgiveness. Because God's love works to reweave humanity and the web of life, reconciliation is a process and not a one-time event, whether in the past, present, or future. Out of God's love, we receive the justification that comes through faith. In this sense, love must be understood as forgiveness. As we continue to reject and deny God's presence in large and small ways throughout our lifetime, God is willing to wipe the slate clean and give us a second, third, or hundred-and-third chance when we respond again to God's forgiving love. Here the distinction between reconciliation and redemption or restoration is helpful. Reconciliation involves God's loving forgiveness toward humanity and humanity's continual growth in love as we respond moment by moment throughout our life. In and through our reconciliation to God, one another, and the created order, the entire web of life — the whole of creation — is restored to a state of flourishing and well-being. In his lectures on Christology, Dietrich Bonhoeffer aptly noted that the created order has no need to reconcile with God or humanity because the source of its brokenness arises out of human self-centeredness, indifference, and carelessness. Our reconciliation with God and one another restores the web of life, in and through the prior reality of God's own love for us, expressed as forgiveness.

Reconciliation and Healing. But reconciliation as justification is incomplete without sanctification or the renewal of the image of God within each of us, in order that we might more fully embody God's love. The "sin-sick soul" in need of God's healing power is a common Christian metaphor. Just as the body needs healing, at times the soul requires the Great Physician to bind our wounds and to set right the brokenness within us. Over time, God's love continues to illuminate the ways in which we are not caring for the body — whether the human body as an individual, the collective body of humanity, or the "body of God" as the whole of creation — and to prescribe for us a new course that can restore these bodies to health. Thus, love works to ferret out and bring to our awareness the ways in which sin — our rejection or denial of God's love — thwarts the reconciliation process that began with God's promises to Abraham, became flesh in Jesus of Nazareth, and continues toward the eventual completion of the new creation. Again and again, our sin turns its back on God, but God's love continues to tap us on the shoulder and reorient us. God's reconciling love desires to heal the wounds of the world.

Reconciliation and Justice. God never forces us to accept the gift of love. Likewise, we cannot force others to accept God's love and cannot, ourselves, act consistently in loving ways. We are called, nonetheless, to participate in God's reconciling love. James Cone has argued that requesting or expecting forgiveness as the ultimate solution to our personal and social wrongs is insufficient. Forgiveness is not only about a change of heart, what we sometimes call "repentance," but also about a changed life in which we participate in reconciliation. Loving justice takes on flesh, reaching out to break open societal standards, to illuminate injustice, and to alleviate suffering. The embodiment of justice is not simply about the privileged reaching out to help the impoverished and marginalized; it also places a demand upon the powerless. Cone argues that reconciliation has both an objective and subjective side: there is what God does in liberating the oppressed, but there is also what the oppressed do in "joining God in the fight against injustice and oppression."[15] In other words, the work of reconciliation is a universal responsibility, as we participate in God's loving justice. This responsibility means that, at times, the privileged take the lower position at the table, empowering the disenfranchised to find voice and self-determination where they have had little or none. At other times, it means that the marginalized must stand for change. For example, in labor unions, farm workers have found voice and strength for pursuing justice and quality-of-life issues. Homeowners situated next to dumping grounds for toxic wastes speak out and take action against the government to ensure their children's health is not compromised. Liberation from injustice and oppression is a universal responsibility that manifests itself in particular life situations and contributes to the reconciliation process.

Luke's parables of the banquet speak volumes about God's love, justice, and preferentiality toward the powerless as part of the reconciliation process: those who are invited to the banquet are "the poor, the cripple, the lame, and the blind" — that is, those who are rejected by society (Luke 14:12). Conversely, those who believe they already have the fullness of life in their possessions and relationships refuse the invitation (Luke 14:16–24). They are not interested in justice, healing, or reconciliation, but prefer the illusion of the good lives that they already possess, or perhaps, they feel threatened or fearful toward society's outcasts. As more than one student, forced to read liberation theology as a part of a systematics course, has asked, "What do the experiences of the poor and marginalized have to do with me? Why should I fight for environmental justice? I haven't done anything to hurt them." However, when we participate in God's love, rather than a lesser love of our own design, we recognize that love is the power of being and that the good life is nothing short of radical relationality.

The Liberating Demand of Love in God

Our discussion of the relationship between reconciliation, love, and justice leads us to consider the liberating demand of love. When our loves and life are reoriented according to God's own love, we participate in the process of reconciling the whole of creation. As the above discussion indicates, the liberating demand entails both a personal component and a social dimension.

Personal Liberation. When we open ourselves to God's love, we are moved to relinquish our misguided and misdirected expressions of eros and philia. Self-serving and selfish love, which stands opposed to agape and seeks to thrive at the expense of others, is reoriented. Where once our loves focused exclusively on personal needs and desires, love becomes other-regarding, mutually upbuilding, and a reflection of God's reconciliation and justice. Love liberates us from ourselves. For example, if we donate our used automobile to charity, not because we have a genuine desire to help, but merely because we receive a tax write-off, our love remains self-serving. Or if we work at the homeless shelter because it makes us feel important or as a result of a court-ordered sentence requiring so many hours of volunteer work in the community, this, too, represents self-serving love, though of course, the process itself has the potential to reorient the person and to serve justice, despite the intentions.

Even so, we should not confuse the self-serving and selfish love that exists apart from God with the self-love that is grounded in and returns to God. The Great Commandment demands that we love the Lord our God with all our heart, soul, strength, and mind, and love our neighbor as ourselves (Luke 10:27). We sometimes overlook that the love of neighbor is intertwined with the love of self; that is, how we love ourselves directly affects our responsibility and actions toward others. While various self-help and popular psychology gurus can give us insight into our behaviors, the source of the full restoration of our humanity is found only in and through God's love. To love ourselves means, to paraphrase Paul Tillich, we must accept that we are accepted. We must open ourselves to the reality of God's love as it calls to us like a lover to its beloved. In the eyes of God, each of us is a precious, beautiful, beloved child — no matter what we do or how miserably we fail to follow God's way, God's love never fails to pursue us and desire the best for us.

The first element of the liberating demand of love is simply this demand to accept that we are beloved by God and that God wants the best for us, in spite of the world that remains enslaved in its loveless, hopeless, and faithless expressions. In other words, it is not enough to believe that God is bringing the new creation into our midst. It is not enough to hope for the full restoration of the web of life. We must also take to heart God's love, which seeks to find a home in each and all of us in the concrete, historical, cultural circumstances of our lives. Paul makes this point when he writes, "For I am convinced that neither death, nor life, nor angels, nor rulers, nor things present, nor things to come, nor powers, nor height, nor depth, nor anything else in all creation, will be able to separate us from the love of God in Christ Jesus our Lord" (Rom. 8:38–39). These powerful words remind us that the only thing capable of preventing God's own love from filling us, reorienting us, and leading us toward the fullness of life is our own free will when it chooses to reject and deny God's love. God's infinite, eternal, radically relational love taps us on the shoulder and raps on the door to our heart, whether or not we respond. When love finds a home, it opens the door to our heart. We invite others in and go out to meet others where they are. Love liberates us from our selfish and self-serving ways.

At the same time, however, love also begins the work of forming the reality of the self before God. The long, complex debate in Western thought over the notion of the self is beyond the scope of this project; nevertheless, we sense that each individual is a separate and integral personal structure. As Christians, we affirm that God created the human being with certain capacities and potential. God intends for each of us to develop and express our full humanity. Unfortunately, the structures of existence suppress and deny the capacities and possibilities present in many persons, and certain groups and segments of our society and world suffer disproportionately at the hands of institutions, the powerful, and the privileged. Thus, even as God's love liberates each person to be fully human before God and with others, the process of self-love manifests itself in various ways. Among the most privileged, self-love means a willingness to be less: less powerful, less wealthy, less important, less the center of attention. Among the most marginalized, self-love means a willingness to discover what it means to be fully human in the context of their own lives and experiences, as well as to find voice and to seek justice. Among the many who live in between the extremes, self-love means a combination of giving away and receiving life. But whoever we are, we can only begin to discover the meaning of being fully human and fully ourselves in the presence of God's liberating love. The process of reconciliation requires that each of us be guided and shaped by the love of God to most fully express our humanity, and human flourishing is a matter of God's way taking shape in us.

Social Liberation. The liberating demand of love, however, does not rest in personal liberation. Liberation from and restoration to ourselves in a spiritual sense is but one component of the liberation demanded by God's love. As discussed previously, we are not to become God or to be mystically fused with God. Rather, our journey is a return to the fullness and goodness of our createdness, as intended by God. The traditional understanding of the resurrection of the body, often dismissed as illogical and unsophisticated, points toward the fact that we remain creatures, even at the completion of the new creation. We are created as embodied and limited beings, not as ethereal, ubiquitous spirits; yet, in the beginning our limits overflowed with the fullness of life. The liberating demand of love necessarily includes a social dimension that encompasses the material world. Here, again, James 2:15–16 strikes us with its pointedness: "If a brother or sister is naked and lacks daily food, and one of you says to them, 'Go in peace; keep warm and eat your fill,' and yet you do not supply their bodily needs, what is the good of that?" The portrait of Jesus addressing physical needs is painted in bold strokes and brilliant colors. Love looks us in the eyes and commands, "Feed my sheep." If the food we provide is spiritual only, the body that was created by God and deemed to be "very good" will perish. If the food is real, both the body and spirit have the means to flourish. Even so, we must understand the food, too, is participating in the process of liberation. When the rich heap high their plates at the all-you-can-eat Food-a-rama Restaurant and throw into the garbage tons of leftovers, while millions of children cry from the gnawing pain of hunger, the radical relationality of the world is thwarted. When we pollute the air and water, the life-sustaining goodness of creation is shackled. But love seeks the well-being of the whole of creation, and all of creation participates in liberation to life.

The liberation that is demanded by God's love is also liberation from harmful and oppressive social structures. As love works in and through us, it demands our participation in opposing what is wrong and destructive and protecting what is right and life-enhancing. In the story of the woman who was "caught in adultery," this understanding unfolds. Jesus was teaching at the temple, and "the scribes and the Pharisees brought a woman who had been caught in adultery" (John 8:3). They remind Jesus that the law commands she be stoned, and we can surmise that the stoning would likely lead to her death. Jesus' response is silence, as he reaches down and writes in the dirt with his finger. "When they kept on questioning him, he straightened up and said to them, 'Let anyone among you who is without sin be the first to throw a stone at her' " (John 8:7). Slowly, one by one, the men depart and leave Jesus "alone with the woman standing before him" (8:9). Rather than condemning her, Jesus sends her on her way, admonishing her not to sin again.

Several features of this story highlight the liberating demand of love as it moves against social constructs and systems of injustice. First, Jesus does not condone the woman's wrongdoing; he clearly commands her not to sin again. Yet Jesus says "no" not only to what is wrong in the case of the women, but also to what is wrong in the case of the powerful and privileged leaders who wish to condemn her. We are not told who the woman's accomplice might have been, whether he was privileged or among the poor. Nevertheless, the leaders have not condemned the man caught in adultery, only the woman. Jesus has no tolerance for a system that condemns the woman to death but allows the man's life to continue unabated. As God's own love in the world, Jesus of Nazareth stands in the face of powerful institutions that give no voice or rights to groups of people based upon physical characteristics, and pushes back against their harmful and destructive ways. The way of God is the way of life. Moreover, as he writes in the dirt, Jesus points to our connection to the earth and one another: we are created from and, in our broken-offness, will return to the earth. Men, women, children, animals, bushes, dirt; we are all woven into this web by the hand of God.

Though the woman remained subject to a system that rendered her powerless, perhaps she was emboldened by her encounter with God's love to pursue liberation and radical relationality. Perhaps she now stood with other women facing destructive situations, like women in Africa joining forces to oppose female circumcision. Perhaps one or two of the leaders who sought to have her stoned was reoriented by his encounter with God's love and, like Saul or Nicodemus, began to relinquish some of his power and privilege to participate in the liberating and reconciling work of love. Perhaps someone might use his power and privilege to bring justice and reconciliation, as did Desmond Tutu in South Africa after apartheid. Love demands our participation in the liberation process within the created world. It reminds us that we are all woven into the fabric of life, and when one person or atom is diminished by the self-serving ways of others, we all suffer. God's love manifests its radically relational reality and demands that we participate in the process.

The Humble Response to Love. When our loves and lives are re-oriented by God's love, then the principle of life becomes central. The gospel, the good news of God's love for humanity in Christ and the Holy Spirit, is a life-centered discourse, promoting the well-being of the whole of creation. Humanity has a particular responsibility for promoting restoration because we bear the lion's share of the culpability. We are commanded, above all else, to love the Lord our God and to love our neighbors as ourselves. Nowhere in the Scriptures do we find the command to judge the Lord our God and to judge our neighbors as we judge ourselves. Instead, we are commanded to love, and love always seeks the life and well-being of the other. If we pause and consider those whom we love, whether family, friends, or pets, our deepest desire is that they live long lives and flourish. Yet this analogy barely scratches the surface of God's love as it seeks our well-being and flourishing. God's love creates, redeems, and sustains life, and we are called to do the same as this love flows through us to the whole of creation.

The life-centered orientation of God's love in the world is never simple; as earlier noted, choosing life is constrained and complicated by the broken-offness that continues to shape life on earth. But as we grow in God's love and respond in loving ways toward creation, we find that, paradoxically, love does not puff us up, but rather leads toward a growing sense of humility. To recognize and uphold the value and interrelatedness of creation is a humbling responsibility. Not only do we realize that apart from God we can do nothing, we also come to accept that our decisions and choices may prove, in time, to be misguided and misdirected. Does choosing life mean prolonging for months or years the bodily functions of a comatose patient? What if I must choose between the best situation for my spouse and the best situation for my aging parents? Does choosing life mean producing lumber for Habitat for Humanity homes or preserving forests? When we choose life, sometimes we find the best choice is not entirely obvious. Sometimes we choose poorly, for we are not God. Usually, we find ourselves unable to discern the full implications of any decision aimed at life. But, in all cases, we remain beloved by God, whose love continues to reach out for us and bring us to a new understanding and expression of God's way in the world, urging us to change, often when we think we are filled with love.

The paradoxical character of love's humility is magnificently expressed in Paul's First Letter to the Corinthians, a passage that stands as one of the greatest in literature. In it Paul reminds us, "Love is patient; love is kind; love is not envious or boastful or arrogant or rude. It does not insist on its own way; it is not irritable or resentful; it does not rejoice in wrongdoing, but rejoices in the truth. It bears all things, believes all things, hopes all things, endures all things. Love never ends" (1 Cor. 13:4–8). God's love is never coercive or demanding, but calls to us and waits for our response. God does not force us, but nudges and invites us. Indeed, it is often said that we can substitute "God" for the word "love" throughout this text, as a means of grasping what it means to truly live in the image of God. Despite the reality of God's radically relational love, which is the very power of being, God respects the integrity of each life and its capacities. There can be little doubt that love is the most powerful force in the universe, despite the strength and durability of evil. Nonetheless, we are humbled when we grasp the gentle ways of love, despite and because of its power.

As Christians, we wager our lives on the prevailing power of love. As followers of God in Christ in the Holy Spirit, we are called to accept, by faith, that God's way is in our best interest. We are urged to travel, by hope, toward the promise of the good life and human flourishing. And we are empowered by love to participate in the destination of God's own love, expressed in the present as a demand that moves us toward the reconciliation and renewal that God will bring to completion in God's time. If we seek the good life and the flourishing of all, then we must choose to participate in these three, which connect us to God and one other, facilitate our Christian journey, and form the Christ-character in us. The three excellences of faith, hope, and love are given to us as gifts, but our ongoing response and participation is demanded. We seek the good life and human flourishing, but we must embody faith, hope, and love in tangible ways, for God in Christ in the Holy Spirit claims the whole of creation as its very own.

EPILOGUE

In faith, hope, and love, we come full circle and return to the beginning. From the Christian perspective, the question of whether we can be good or inhabit the good life without God is answered in the negative. If we do not participate in God in Christ in the Holy Spirit, our journey will come up short. Faith, hope, and love enable us to participate in God and to pursue the good life found in the flourishing of the whole of creation. Ours is a time of uncertainty — a time when faith, hope, and love sometimes seem to be little more than the wishful thinking of our more primitive ancestors or the myriad expressions of human needs and desires. As post-Enlightenment people, we cannot return to a more innocent time, intellectually or spiritually. Yet like every Christian who has traveled this road before us, we are faced with a choice: either we accept the reality of God in Christ in the Holy Spirit and embrace its particular way of being in the world, or we resign ourselves to living by means of our own devices apart from God's grace. The lifelines of faith, hope, and love are offered to all, but we must open ourselves to receive and embody them amid the particular circumstances of our lives. These three are the ties that bind us to God and enable us to participate in God. When we choose this alternative reality as the "really real" choice, our spiritual senses become reoriented and redirected in significant ways.

The Universal and the Particular

Our lifelines to God open us to a sense of balance between the universal and the particular, the immanent and the transcendent. Earlier

generations of theologians have depicted these pairs in terms of "polarities" and "tensions," which carried the sense of being pulled in
two directions simultaneously. The Western philosophical tradition
generally seeks resolution to such tensions and paradoxes, rather
than dwelling within them. Perhaps we can learn something from
the yin and yang of the East, in which seemingly opposite qualities
or concepts are held in balance and harmony, as they strengthen one
another. As universal gifts of the Spirit, faith, hope, and love are available to all persons, regardless of any physical, historical, or cultural
characteristics, yet because we live as finite people in specific contexts, these three take shape in particular ways within our lives. An
elderly woman living in rural Kenya faces distinctive circumstances in
which her faith, hope, and love find expression — so, too, the young
Latino struggling to make ends meet in the *colonias* along the border
of Texas and Mexico. We recognize that, in following God in Christ
in the Holy Spirit, these three become embodied in specific configura-
tions of time, space, and culture; even so, they remain the basic gifts
of grace enabling us to participate in God.

Difference in Unity

Although faith, hope, and love are universal gifts of God in Christ
in the Holy Spirit and different aspects of the one same grace, they
each play a distinctive role in our spiritual journey. At times, we find
it difficult to differentiate among the three and, indeed, they over-
lap and intertwine, yet together these three excellences empower our
journey and form the Christ-character in us. Faith is accepting that
God's way is in our best interest, despite "evidence" or assertions to
the contrary. Hope is the momentum and direction for our journey;
when life's possibilities seem to narrow, hope opens a door or un-
covers a new trail that enables us to continue following after God in
Christ in the Holy Spirit. Love is the radically relational reality we
seek and that seeks us across the landscape of our lives; it is a destination where reconciliation and renewal are realized. When we embody
and express all three of these gifts of grace, we are confronted with

the liberating demand that calls us to act in specific ways as we participate in the promised renewal of all things. The liberating demand of faith, hope, and love also requires us to renounce our previous self-interested and self-serving ways.

Radical Relationality

As we turn away from our self-centered existence and reorient our lives and loves in God, we participate in the reality of God at work in the world, reweaving the threads of existence and restoring a radical relationality among the whole of creation. As Christians, we recognize that the fabric of existence is, indeed, frayed. Yet at the same time, we catch glimpses of the hand of God as it reweaves the fabric. Faith, hope, and love are radically relational qualities; they come to us as a threesome, and our lives depend upon the three working together for the approaching goodness and flourishing of life. God in Christ in the Holy Spirit is a radically relational reality, even though we struggle to understand the height, breadth, and depth of this triune God. Although we currently live in the broken-offness of human life together and drag the rest of creation into the muck, the end of our journey promises to be a radically transformed and renewed existence, premised upon radical relationality. God, humanity, and the whole of creation will be woven again into a complex, exquisite, life-giving tapestry.

The Good Life Revisited

When we return to our opening chapter and the question of whether we can be good without God or can discover the good life by our own efforts, it thus becomes evident that we must renew the spiritual dimension of life together. We struggle against the loss of social capital in North America and the decline of participation in communities. We find it difficult to deny that the American spirit seems increasingly to be a spirit of the self. We rail against churches focused upon either self-improvement or self-preservation. We yearn to participate in something more. We yearn for life in its fullness. *These three* open us to the reality of God and invite our participation in that reality; they offer us access to something more. But faith, hope, and love are not some secret door to another world, as depicted in C. S. Lewis's *Narnia Chronicles;* they are the basic qualities or attributes that begin to form the Christ-character in us.

The Christ-character is best understood as the fullest expression of what it means to be human in the midst of radical relationship with God, others, and creation. Although we can develop and refine certain intellectual skills and strive to be moral, ethical people, the pervasive reality of sin and broken-offness means that limits exist to both knowledge and ethics. Our flourishing as human beings requires a radical transformation of the structures of existence, the web of all living things, and each of us. The good life can be found, or at least it can caress our cheek in the midst of the world, but it depends upon the present and promised renewal of the whole of creation. These three — faith, hope, and love — are the ties that bind us to God and one another; they are the heart of the Christ-character taking shape in the world. Our participation in God and the radical renewal of life depends on them taking shape in us, as the living and breathing body of Christ in time, space, and culture.

NOTES

Chapter One: Is the Fabric Frayed?

1. David G. Myers, *The American Paradox: Spiritual Hunger in an Age of Plenty* (New Haven and London: Yale University Press, 2000), xi.

2. Ibid.

3. Robert D. Putnam, *Bowling Alone: The Collapse and Revival of American Community* (New York: Simon & Schuster, 2000), 19.

4. Robert N. Bellah, "The Protestant Structure of American Culture: Multiculture or Monoculture?" *Hedgehog Review* 4, no. 1 (Spring 2002): 17.

5. Myers, *The American Paradox*, 3ff.

6. Andrew Delbanco, *The Real American Dream* (Cambridge, Mass.: Harvard University Press, 1999), 91.

7. Bellah, "The Protestant Structure of American Culture," 10.

8. Ibid., 22.

9. Ibid., 18, 20.

10. Myers, *The American Paradox*, 270.

11. Ibid., 267.

12. Wade Clark Roof, *Spiritual Marketplace: Baby Boomers and the Remaking of American Religion* (Princeton, N.J.: Princeton University Press, 1999), 318.

13. Martin Marty, "Young Clergy: Where Are They?" *Sightings* (Martin Marty Center of the University of Chicago), March 26, 2001.

14. Laurie Goodstein, "Search for the Right Church Ends at Home," *New York Times*, April 29, 2001, A1.

15. Bellah, "The Protestant Structure of American Culture," 12.

16. Thomas Merton, *Thoughts in Solitude* (London: Burns & Oates, 1958), 70.

Chapter Two: These Three in Historical Perspective

1. My use of the phrase "experience of God" in no way implies that our relationship with the divine is based solely upon "feeling" or "emotions," because our experience of God can include the wilderness times or, as Saint

John of the Cross expresses, the dark nights of the soul. Rather, the experience of God should be understood as an openness to and awareness of the reality of God as an integral part of our existence.

2. Edward Farley, *Deep Symbols: Their Postmodern Effacement and Reclamation* (Valley Forge, Pa.: Trinity Press International, 1996), 3.

3. Ibid., 5.

4. Joseph Campbell, *Myths to Live By: How We Re-Create Ancient Legends in Our Daily Lives to Release Human Potential* (New York: Penguin, 1972).

5. Marcus J. Borg, *Reading the Bible Again for the First Time* (San Francisco: HarperSanFrancisco, 2001), 29.

6. Alasdair MacIntyre, *After Virtue: A Study in Moral Theory,* 2nd ed. (Notre Dame, Ind.: University of Notre Dame Press, 1984), 106–8.

7. For an accessible and more complete introduction to the virtues and Greek ethics, see William J. Prior, *Virtue and Knowledge* (London and New York: Routledge, 1991).

8. Aristotle, *The Nichomachean Ethics,* in *The Complete Works of Aristotle,* vol. 2, ed. Jonathan Barnes (Princeton, N.J.: Princeton University Press, 1984), 1731 (I:5, 1095b 26–27).

9. Ibid., 1862 (X:7, 1178a 5–8).

10. Ibid., 1860–61 (X:7, 1177a 20–23).

11. Ibid., 1748 (II:6, 1107a 1).

12. Ibid., 1747 (II:6, 1106b 31–32).

13. Saint Augustine, *The Enchiridion on Faith, Hope, and Love* (Washington, D.C.: Regnery Publishing, 1961), 3.

14. Saint Augustine, *The City of God* (New York: Penguin Books, 1972), 195 (V:10).

15. Ibid., 412 (X:28).

16. Ibid., 431 (XI:3).

17. Ibid., 196 (V:11).

18. Ibid., 857 (XIX:4).

19. Ibid., 852 (XIX:4).

20. Etienne Gilson, *The Christian Philosophy of St. Thomas Aquinas* (New York: Random House, 1956), 303.

21. Thomas Aquinas, *Disputed Questions on Virtue: Quaestio Disputata de Virtutibus in Communi* and *Quaestio Disputata de Virtutibus Cardinalibus,* trans. Ralph McInerny (South Bend, Ind.: St. Augustine's Press, 1999), 60 (Art. 9, Ad 7).

22. Gilson, *The Christian Philosophy of St. Thomas Aquinas,* 338.

23. *Disputed Questions on Virtue,* 89 (Art. 12).

Chapter Three: Faith in God

1. Ray Kurzweil, *The Age of Spiritual Machines* (New York: Viking Penguin, 1999), 2.

2. Paul Tillich, *Dynamics of Faith* (New York: Harper & Row, 1957).

3. Robert N. Bellah, "The Protestant Structure of American Culture: Multiculture or Monoculture?" *Hedgehog Review* 4, no. 1 (Spring 2002): 22.

4. Bruce H. Wilkinson, *The Prayer of Jabez* (Sisters, Ore.: Multnomah Publications, 2000).

5. For further discussion of the Prayer of Jabez in light of the Lord's Prayer, see Rodney Clapp and John Wright, "God as Santa: Misreading the Prayer of Jabez," *Christian Century* 119, no. 22 (October 23–November 5, 2002): 29–31.

6. Wilkinson, *The Prayer of Jabez*, 79ff.

7. Barbara Brown Taylor, "One Step at a Time," *The Preaching Life* (Cambridge, Mass.: Cowley, 1993), 93.

Chapter Four: Hope in God

1. The use of the world "topography" is intended as an acknowledgment that the following meditation represents a description of our experiences of contemporary life and not a metaphysical rendering of the structures of reality in and of themselves.

2. Heinz Zahrnt, *The Question of God* (New York: Harcourt Brace Jovanovich, 1966), provides an excellent account of the modern theologians who wrestled with the marginalization of God in the midst of cultural Protestantism and Protestant liberalism and a world beset by wars of unprecedented magnitude.

3. This claim is not intended as a criticism, but rather as a way of recognizing the iterative nature of theological discourse. Over time and further reflection, we come to see weaknesses in our understanding of God and the journey of faith, as well as the changes in historical and cultural contexts, and we readjust our course headings.

4. Stephen Hawking, *A Brief History of Time*, updated ed. (New York: Bantam Books, 1996), 34.

5. Jennifer Trusted, *Physics and Metaphysics: Theories of Space and Time* (London: Routledge, 1991), 177.

6. Bella Thomas, "What the World's Poor Watch on TV," *World Press Review* 50, no. 3 (March 2003): 30.

7. Paul Tillich, *Systematic Theology* (Chicago: University of Chicago Press, 1963), 3:129.

8. Ibid., 3:135.

9. Ibid., 3:155ff.

10. Ibid., 3:129.

11. Ibid., 1:64, 196.

12. Ibid., 2:12.

13. Paul Tillich, *The Courage to Be* (New Haven and London: Yale University Press, 1952), 1.

14. "Otherness" or "the other" often teeters precariously on the precipice of becoming an ontological category, rather than serving to speak of our imperative to recognize, respect, and be affected by particularity and diversity as it takes shape in real people and communities.

15. David Carr, *Time, Narrative, and History* (Bloomington: Indiana University Press, 1986), 4.

16. Adam Kuper, *Culture: The Anthropologists' Account* (Cambridge, Mass.: Harvard University Press, 1999), 227.

17. See, for example, Michael Hardt and Antonio Negri, *Empire* (Cambridge, Mass.: Harvard University Press, 2000), and Zygmunt Bauman, *Globalization: The Human Consequences* (Cambridge, U.K.: Polity, 1998).

18. Bauman, *Globalization,* 73.

19. Ibid.

20. Ibid., 76.

21. Edward Farley, *Deep Symbols: Their Postmodern Effacement and Reclamation* (Valley Forge, Pa.: Trinity Press International, 1996), 57.

22. Dorothee Sölle, *Thinking about God: An Introduction to Theology* (Valley Forge, Pa.: Trinity Press International, 1990), 51.

23. Farley, *Deep Symbols,* 98.

24. Delores S. Williams, *Sisters in the Wilderness: The Challenge of Womanist God-Talk* (Maryknoll, N.Y.: Orbis Books, 1993), 108–39.

25. "follow, *v.*" *Oxford English Dictionary,* ed. J. A. Simpson and E. S. C. Weiner, 2nd ed. (Oxford: Clarendon Press, 1989). *OED Online.* Oxford University Press, 2002.

26. Glenn Tinder, *The Fabric of Hope: An Essay* (Atlanta: Scholars Press, 1999), 28.

27. Paul Ricoeur, "The Hermeneutics of Testimony," *Essays on Biblical Interpretation* (Philadelphia: Fortress Press, 1980), 131ff.

28. Paul Ricoeur, "Hope and the Structure of Philosophical Systems," *Figuring the Sacred: Religion, Narrative, and Imagination* (Minneapolis: Fortress Press, 1995), 208.

29. Ibid., 206–7.

30. Paul Ricoeur, "Naming God," *Figuring the Sacred,* 225.

31. Ricoeur, "Freedom in the Light of Hope," *Essays on Biblical Interpretation,* 162.

32. Paul Ricoeur, "Rhetoric-Poetics-Hermeneutics," in *From Metaphysics to Rhetoric,* ed. Michel Meyer (Dordrecht: Kluwer Academic Publishers, 1989), 143.

33. Rebecca S. Chopp, "Reimagining Public Discourse," in *Black Faith and Public Talk,* ed. Dwight N. Hopkins (Maryknoll, N.Y.: Orbis Books, 1999), 157.

34. Ibid.

35. Ibid., 158.

36. Ricoeur, "Naming God," 228.

Chapter Five: Love in God

1. For an excellent treatment of the way eros has been opposed to agape in theology, see Josef Pieper, "Love," in *Faith-Hope-Love* (San Francisco: Ignatius Press, 1997), 210–16.

2. Gottfried Quell and Ethelbert Stauffer, "Love," *Bible Key Words from Gerhard Kittel's Theologisches Wörterbuch zum Neuen Testament* (London: Adam and Charles Black, 1949), 25.

3. Plato, "Symposium," in *Plato: The Collected Dialogues,* ed. Edith Hamilton and Huntington Cairns (Princeton, N.J.: Princeton University Press, 1989), 562 (211b).

4. Ibid., 558 (206a–206e).

5. Aristotle, "Metaphysics," in *The Complete Works of Aristotle,* Revised Oxford Translation, ed. Jonathan Barnes, vol. 2 (Princeton, N.J.: Princeton University Press, 1984), 1694–95 (1072b:30).

6. Martha C. Nussbaum, *The Fragility of Goodness* (Cambridge: Cambridge University Press, 1986), 354.

7. Ibid.

8. Not only do Nygren and Barth focus on eros and agape, but so, too, does Pieper, even as he argues for the place of eros in the Christian life. Likewise, Quell and Stauffer devote merely two sentences to philia, but three pages each to eros and agape.

9. Ada María Isasi-Díaz, *Mujerista Theology* (Maryknoll, N.Y.: Orbis Books, 1996), 89.

10. Nussbaum, *The Fragility of Goodness,* 355.

11. Quell and Stauffer, "Love," 28.

12. Pieper, "Love," 222.

13. Martha C. Nussbaum, *Upheavals of Thought: The Intelligence of Emotions* (Cambridge: Cambridge University Press, 2001), 322–23.

14. Ibid., 237.

15. James H. Cone, *God of the Oppressed,* new rev. ed. (Maryknoll, N.Y.: Orbis Books, 1997), 213.

SELECT BIBLIOGRAPHY

Aquinas, Thomas. *Disputed Questions on Virtue.* Trans. Ralph McInerny. South Bend, Ind.: St. Augustine's Press, 1999.

Aristotle. *Metaphysics.* Trans. W. D. Ross. *The Complete Works of Aristotle.* Vol. 2. Ed. Jonathan Barnes. Princeton, N.J.: Princeton University Press, 1984.

———. *The Nichomachean Ethics.* Trans. W. D. Ross. *The Complete Works of Aristotle.* Vol. 2. Ed. Jonathan Barnes. Princeton, N.J.: Princeton University Press, 1984.

Augustine. *City of God.* Trans. Henry Bettenson. New York: Penguin Books, 1984.

———. *The Confessions of St. Augustine.* Trans. John K. Ryan. New York: Doubleday, 1960.

———. *The Enchiridion on Faith, Hope, and Love.* Trans. S. B. Shaw. Washington, D.C.: Regnery Publishing, 1961.

Bauman, Zygmunt. *Globalization: The Human Consequences.* Cambridge, U.K.: Polity, 1998.

Bellah, Robert N. "The Protestant Structure of American Culture: Multiculture or Monoculture?" *Hedgehog Review* 4, no. 1 (Spring 2002): 7–28.

Bonhoeffer, Dietrich. *Christ the Center.* San Francisco: Harper & Row, 1978.

———. *Letters and Papers from Prison.* Enlarged ed. Ed. Eberhard Bethge. New York: Macmillan Publishing Company, 1971.

Borg, Marcus. *Reading the Bible Again for the First Time.* San Francisco: HarperSanFrancisco, 2001.

Campbell, Joseph. *Myths to Live By: How We Re-Create Ancient Legends in Our Daily Lives to Release Human Potential.* New York: Penguin, 1972.

Carr, David. *Time, Narrative, and History.* Bloomington: Indiana University Press, 1986.

Chopp, Rebecca S. "Reimagining Public Discourse." In *Black Faith and Public Talk.* Ed. Dwight N. Hopkins. Maryknoll, N.Y.: Orbis Books, 1999.

Clapp, Rodney, and John Wright. "God as Santa: Misreading the Prayer of Jabez." *Christian Century* 119, no. 22 (October 23–November 5, 2002): 29–31.

Cone, James H. *God of the Oppressed.* Rev. ed. Maryknoll, N.Y.: Orbis Books, 1997.

Delbanco, Andrew. *The Real American Dream.* Cambridge, Mass.: Harvard University Press, 1999.

Farley, Edward. *Deep Symbols: Their Postmodern Effacement and Reclamation.* Valley Forge, Pa.: Trinity Press International, 1996.

Gilson, Etienne. *The Christian Philosophy of St. Thomas Aquinas.* New York: Random House, 1956.

Goodstein, Laurie. "Search for the Right Church Ends at Home." *New York Times,* April 29, 2001: A1.

Hardt, Michael, and Antonio Negri. *Empire.* Cambridge, Mass.: Harvard University Press, 2000.

Hawking, Stephen. *A Brief History of Time.* Updated ed. New York: Bantam Books, 1988 and 1996.

Isasi-Díaz, Ada María. *Mujerista Theology.* Maryknoll, N.Y.: Orbis Books, 1996.

Kuper, Adam. *Culture: The Anthropologists' Account.* Cambridge, Mass.: Harvard University Press, 1999.

Kurzweil, Ray. *The Age of Spiritual Machines.* New York: Viking Penguin, 1999.

Marty, Martin. "Young Clergy: Where Are They?" *Sightings* (March 26, 2001). Chicago: Martin Marty Center of the University of Chicago.

McFague, Sallie. *The Body of God: An Ecological Theology.* Minneapolis: Fortress Press, 1993.

MacIntyre, Alasdair. *After Virtue: A Study in Moral Theory.* 2nd ed. Notre Dame, Ind.: University of Notre Dame Press, 1984.

Merton, Thomas. *Thoughts in Solitude.* London: Burns & Oates, 1958.

Moltmann, Jürgen. *Theology of Hope.* Minneapolis: Fortress Press, 1993.

Myers, David G. *The American Paradox: Spiritual Hunger in an Age of Plenty.* New Haven and London: Yale University Press, 2000.

Niebuhr, H. Richard. *Christ and Culture.* New York: Harper, 1951.

Nussbaum, Martha C. *The Fragility of Goodness.* Cambridge: Cambridge University Press, 1986.

———. *Upheavals of Thought: The Intelligence of Emotions.* Cambridge: Cambridge University Press, 2001.

Pieper, Josef. *Faith-Hope-Love.* San Francisco: Ignatius Press, 1997.

Plato. *The Republic.* Trans. Paul Shorey. In *Plato: The Collected Dialogues.* Ed. Edith Hamilton and Huntington Cairns. Princeton, N.J.: Princeton University Press, 1989.

———. *Symposium.* Trans. Michael Joyce. In *Plato: The Collected Dialogues.* Ed. Edith Hamilton and Huntington Cairns. Princeton, N.J.: Princeton University Press, 1989.

Prior, William J. *Virtue and Knowledge: An Introduction to Ancient Greek Ethics.* London and New York: Routledge, 1991.

Putnam, Robert D. *Bowling Alone: The Collapse and Revival of American Community.* New York: Simon & Schuster, 2000.

Quell, Gottfried, and Ethelbert Stauffer. "Love." *Bible Key Words from Gerhard Kittel's Theologisches Wörterbuch zum Neuen Testament.* Trans. and ed. J. R. Coates. London: Adam and Charles Black, 1949.

Ricoeur, Paul. *Essays on Biblical Interpretation.* Philadelphia: Fortress Press, 1980.

———. *Figuring the Sacred: Religion, Narrative, and Imagination.* Trans. David Pellauer. Minneapolis: Fortress Press, 1995.

———. "Rhetoric-Poetics-Hermeneutics," *From Metaphysics to Rhetoric.* Ed. Michel Meyer. Trans. Robert Harvey. Dordrecht: Kluwer Academic Publishers, 1989.

Roof, Wade Clark. *Spiritual Marketplace: Baby Boomers and the Remaking of American Religion.* Princeton, N.J.: Princeton University Press, 1999.

Sölle, Dorothee. *Thinking about God: An Introduction to Theology.* Valley Forge, Pa.: Trinity Press International, 1990.

Taylor, Barbara Brown. *The Preaching Life.* Cambridge, Mass.: Cowley, 1993.

Tillich, Paul. *The Courage to Be.* New Haven and London: Yale University Press, 1952.

———. *Dynamics of Faith.* New York: Harper & Row, 1957.

———. *Love, Power, and Justice.* London and New York: Oxford, 1954.

———. *Systematic Theology.* 3 vols. Chicago: University of Chicago Press, 1951, 1957, and 1963.

Tinder, Glenn. *The Fabric of Hope: An Essay.* Atlanta: Scholars Press, 1999.

Trusted, Jennifer. *Physics and Metaphysics: Theories of Space and Time.* London: Routledge, 1991.

Wilkinson, Bruce H. *The Prayer of Jabez.* Sisters, Ore.: Multnomah Publications, 2000.

Williams, Delores S. *Sisters in the Wilderness: The Challenge of Womanist God-Talk.* Maryknoll, N.Y.: Orbis Books, 1993.

Zahrnt, Heinz. *The Question of God.* New York: Harcourt Brace Jovanovich, 1966.

INDEX

reason, 12, 16, 25, 40–41, 43–45,
    47, 57, 88
reformation, 8, 39, 65
relationality, relationship, 21, 23,
    18, 111, 113, 146–48, 161
    of faith, hope, and love, 50–51
relativism, 7, 63, 92
relativity, 57, 91–92, 94
Ricoeur, Paul, 33, 120, 122–23

Saint John of the Cross, 37, 70,
    130
sanctification, 79, 149
science (technology), 57, 88,
    94–95
    and faith, 54–56
    and hope, 87
    and progress, 31
    and time, 91, 93
scripture, 103, 109, 111–12,
    145
    Augustine on, 45–46
    and Christian life, 29, 51
    interpretation of, 34–38, 59
    as life-centered discourse, 73
    and reality, 27–30, 33
    and scientific worldview, 57–58
self, 4, 62, 88, 92, 96
    self-interest, 4, 16, 20, 79, 140,
        143, 148, 150–51, 161
    selflessness, 62, 72
sexuality, 128, 130, 132–33
sin, 4, 14–15, 19–20, 154
    collective, 16–18, 30
    defined, 14

sin (*continued*)
    original, 44, 46–47
    power of, 9, 17, 44, 46, 48
social capital, 3–4, 9, 16, 56, 96,
    135, 161
solidarity, 133–35, 137, 141–42
Sölle, Dorothee, 113
spirituality, 12–13, 21–23, 25, 33,
    35–38, 78–79
    spiritual senses, 25, 75, 159
suffering, 10–11, 46, 74, 82,
    122–25, 143–44

testimony (witness), 120–23
theodicy, 105–6
theological virtues
    Aquinas on, 48–49
    defined, 24
Tillich, Paul, 21, 54, 56–57, 110,
    146, 151
    on courage, 97–99
    and scripture, 26–27
Tinder, Glenn, 119

universality, 13, 22, 45, 138–39,
    150, 159–60

virtue, 39–49
    defined, 50
    problem of usage, 49–50

Wesley, John, 76
Williams, Delores, 117–18

xenophobia, 136–37

Other titles available from
The Pilgrim Press...

DEEP IN THE FAMILIAR
Four Life Rhythms
Joan Cannon Borton

Deep in the Familiar reinterprets the four traditional Hindu life phases into four life rhythms for women viewed through the Christian experience. A woman who explores her life's path with an awareness of these rhythms can become more fully awake to the sacred nature of her daily life.

ISBN 0-8298-1408-6
Paper, 192 pages, $16.00

TRANSFORMING THE ORDINARY
Caroline A. Westerhoff
Foreword by John H. Westerhoff

Westerhoff, a gifted storyteller, uses her talents to create an inspirational collection of essays that will encourage meditation and prayer while enticing readers to view their own everyday worlds in a new light, "anticipating peeks into heaven and brushes up against God."

ISBN 0-8298-1476-0
Paper, 96 pages, $10.00

IN WISDOM'S PATH
Discovering the Sacred in Every Season
Jan L. Richardson

Author and artist Richardson skillfully weaves words to form a tapestry. By following Wisdom's path through the seasons of the church year, readers will discover and share in a deeper meaning of their spirituality.

ISBN 0-8298-1324-1
Paper, 128 pages, $23.00

HENRI'S MANTLE
100 Meditations on Nouwen's Legacy
Chris Glaser

In biblical terms, *mantle* is the equivalent of legacy. Henri Nouwen's mantle consists of more than forty books on how to cultivate a spiritual life. Glaser, a student and friend of Nouwen for over twenty-five years, presents a hundred meditations on Nouwen's words, in the hope that his ministry will continue to thrive.

ISBN 0-8298-1497-3
Paper, 208 pages, $18.00

LABYRINTH AND THE SONG OF SONGS
Jill Kimberly Hartwell Geoffrion

A unique spiritual experience — the fourth in Geoffrion's labyrinth series — cleverly intertwining traditional labyrinthine concepts and the entire Hebrew Scriptures love poem "Song of Songs." For the seasoned labyrinth aficionado who wants to take the next step, spiritually speaking.

ISBN 0-8298-1539-2
Paper, 100 pages, $12.00

NOT RELIGION, BUT LOVE
Practicing a Radical Spirituality of Compassion
Dave Andrews

A liberation spirituality that draws upon the "Christi-Anarchy" concepts — a lifestyle characterized by the radical nonviolent sacrificial compassion of Jesus the Christ. Andrews shows readers how Christ's vision can be put into practice in the communities in which we live. Contains anecdotes, biblical examples, and real-life experiences.

ISBN 0-8298-1546-5
Paper, 208 pages, $16.00

ENCOUNTERS WITH
THE EVER-PRESENT GOD
Howard W. Roberts

Roberts illustrates how biblical stories intersect with contemporary life by teaching readers to pray meaningfully and look at the lives of biblical characters who struggled with their faith. The book explores biblical accounts of how God came to those people and then builds bridges from the biblical lives to contemporary lives.

ISBN 0-8298-1435-3
Paper, 144 pages, $12.00

LIVING THE LABYRINTH
101 Paths to a Deeper Connection with the Sacred
Jill Kimberly Hartwell Geoffrion

This book offers beginners and seasoned labyrinth users a multitude of new ways to approach this sacred tool. The short, devotional-like chapters may be used however the reader chooses — because any way that the labyrinth is approached is the right way.

ISBN 0-8298-1372-1
Paper, 88 pages, $17.00

OUTSIDE THE LINES
Meditations on an Expansive God
Andrea La Sonde Anastos

A collection of meditations that will encourage those looking for a more meaningful relationship with God to discover that "the Holy One who creates and cherishes a universe filled with anteaters and supernovas, with sea anemones and solar systems, will speak to every human being in a unique voice."

ISBN 0-8298-1471-X
Paper, 160 pages, $13.00

PONDERING THE LABYRINTH
Questions to Pray on the Path
Jill Kimberly Hartwell Geoffrion

Designed as a tool for those who are just learning about the labyrinth or those who use it frequently, *Pondering the Labyrinth* is a practical resource that provides hundreds of questions to help individuals embrace their spiritual journey.

ISBN 0-8298-1575-9
Paper, 112 pages, $12.00

PRAYING THE LABYRINTH
A Journal for Spiritual Exploration
Jill Kimberly Hartwell Geoffrion

This book is a journal that leads readers into the spiritual exercise of self-discovery through scripture selections, journaling questions, and poetry, with generous space for personal reflections.

ISBN 0-8298-1343-8
Paper, 112 pages, $15.00

To order these or any other books from
The Pilgrim Press, call or write:

THE PILGRIM PRESS
700 Prospect Avenue
Cleveland, OH 44115-1100

Phone orders: 800-537-3394
(M-F, 8:30am–4:30pm ET)
Fax orders: 216-736-2206

Please include shipping charges
of $4.00 for the first book and
75¢ for each additional book.

Or order from our Web site at
www.pilgrimpress.com.

Prices subject to change without notice.